Recess Is Over

A Handbook for Managing Youthful Offenders in Adult Systems

Barry Glick, Ph.D., NCC
and William Sturgeon, MA

American Correctional Association
Lanham, Maryland

Printed in the United States of America by Graphic Communications Inc.,
Upper Marlboro, Maryland.

For information on publications and videos available from ACA, contact our worldwide web hom page at: http://www.aca.org or www.corrections.com\aca

ISBN 1-56991-143-6

This publication may be ordered from:
American Correctional Association
4380 Forbes Boulevard
Lanham, Maryland 20706-4322
1-800-222-5646

Library of Congress Cataloging-in-Publication Data

Glick, Barry

Recess is Over: a handbook for managing youthful offenders in adult systems / Barry Glick
p. cm.
Includes bibliographical references and index.
ISBN 1-56991-143-6 (pbk.)

1. Juvenile corrections--United States. 2. Prison administration--United States. I. Title

HV9104 .G59 2001

365'.6'083--dc21 2001034322

Table of Contents

ACKNOWLEDGMENTS

This book is the product of many people's efforts. We have been blessed and privileged to traverse this great nation and explore with our colleagues, how public policy concerning youthful offenders in adult correctional systems has been implemented in a variety of settings. We have learned from a great many people: corrections staff such as correctional officers, administrators, supervisors, educators, and support personnel; and from youths, both those incarcerated in penal institutions, those who have served time and have been paroled, and those who have committed some significant antisocial behavior, but have not been caught. We euphemistically refer to the latter as "youths at risk." We have learned from our colleagues, those who have been charged with implementing the policy to incarcerate youths in adult corrections systems. We have learned from our mentors, our friends, our family, and those who have been bold to express their opinions to us, even if unsolicited. All of these individuals have our gratitude and appreciation.

Specific individuals we must mention by name, for they have greatly influenced our work, thoughts, ideas, and this product. Some have done so directly by reading several iterations of the manuscript; some have done so by their own work; and some have been our sounding board for ideas and thinking. To all of you, we shall be indebted for making this book a reality, and the best it could possibly be. In no particular order, our kudos to:

Chief Executive Officers:

- Richard Stalder, past president of ACA and secretary, Louisiana Department of Public Safety and Corrections
- Michael Moore, secretary, Florida Department of Corrections
- Edward "Ned" Loughram, executive director, Council of Junvenile Correctional Administrators
- John Suthers, former director, Colorado Department of Corrections
- Martin Horn, secretary, Governor's Office of Administration, Commonwealth of Pennsylvania
- Joseph Lehman, director, Washington Department of Corrections
- Wayne Scott, former executive director, Texas Department of Criminal Justice
- Gary Johnson, director, Texas Department of Criminal Justice - Institutions
- Jackie Crawford, director, Nevada Department of Prisons
- James L. Saffle, former director, Oklahoma Department of Corrections
- Margaret M. Pugh, commissioner, Alaska Department of Corrections
- Allen Cooper, director, Alaska Department of Corrections
- Mary West, associate director, Colorado Department of Corrections
- Gino Natalucci-Persichetti, director, Ohio Department of Youth Services and chair, Commission on Accreditation for Corrections

Program Directors and Managers

- Kathy Thompson, South Carolina Department of Corrections

- Rufus "BJ" Johnson, South Carolina Department of Corrections
- Diana Coates, Texas Department of Criminal Justice
- Brian Gomez, Colorado Department of Corrections
- Jeaneene Miller, Colorado Department of Corrections
- J. Barry Johnson, Pennsylvania Department of Corrections
- Kathleen M. Kaatz, Clallam Bay Corrections Center, Washington Department of Corrections
- Connie Roehrich, Minnesota Corrections Facility at Shakopee
- Julie Angeles, Minnesota Corrections Facility at Shakopee
- Scott Patterson, West Virginia Division of Corrections
- Sherman Hatcher, Nevada Department of Prisons
- Garland Armstrong, Alaska Department of Corrections

COLLEAGUES

Dr. Arnold P. Goldstein, Syracuse University
Dr. Donald Andrews, Carleton University
Dr. Paul Gendreau, formerly New Brunswick University
Dr. Edward Latessa, University of Cincinnati
Dr. Edward Rhine, Ohio Department of Rehabilitation and Correction
Dr. John Bush, Vermont Department of Corrections
Dr. Juliana Taymans, George Washington University, Washington, D.C.
Nancy Shomaker, National Institute of Corrections Academy, Colorado
William Kearney, former vice president for youth services, Boys and Girls Clubs of America

We certainly are grateful to the American Correctional Association for their vision and leadership in this most important arena. Their support in our work is most influential to the field. Our esteem for James A. Gondles, Jr., CAE, executive director of ACA and Gabriella Daley, director of publications, for their assistance, direction, and encouragement is surpassed only by our gratitude.

Last but not least, we thank Alice Fins, publications managing editor for the American Correctional Association. She has been the catalyst for us to develop and finish this work. Her prodding, questioning, and unyielding position to make this a user-friendly, down-to-earth, no-nonsense, practical and useful resource for the field has challenged us to strive for the best. Michael Kelly, associate editor for this book, has been remarkable in his own insights, staff support, and persistence in assuring our words communicated exactly what we intended. To both of you, our affection, respect, and admiration.

Barry Glick and *William "Bill" Sturgeon*

Foreword

By James A. Gondles, Jr., CAE

Executive Director
American Correctional Association

The following statement concluded the 1998 annual report of the Office of Juvenile Justice and Delinquency Prevention:

"Criminal corrections will also feel the results of the changing juvenile transfer policies. Several states already are struggling to deal with the increased youth population in their prison and jail systems. These systems are not equipped to handle the special needs of young offenders, including educational services, nutritional requirements, and separation from adult criminals. Some states (such as Colorado) have set up separate corrections systems for young offenders, defined as those persons in the criminal justice system who are younger than age twenty-one. As this population increases, states face the task of developing programs to prepare these individuals for release to the community. States also need to train corrections staff who generally deal only with adults, to work with youth. The administrators and directors of corrections systems are looking to other states and the federal government for assistance and guidance in dealing with young offenders."

This work explains how administrators and staff can meet the challenges described above. The authors, Barry Glick and Bill Sturgeon, not only present the problems associated with this population but accompany them with the solutions. Based on their extensive professional experience and consulting work in this field, they provide specific recommendations on planning, staffing, and training that correctional administrators and staff can implement. This text includes a historical context for the current concerns and concludes with a future-oriented goal setting plan. The chapter on the planning module can be used in other situations as well.

After publishing *No Time to Play: Youthful Offenders in Adult Correctional Systems* three years ago, it became apparent that correctional agencies needed more information on the management issues surrounding this unique population. ACA is pleased to offer this handbook to the field. We welcome the input of practitioners and academicians and invite you to publish with us, either in our award-winning magazine, *Corrections Today*, our journal *Corrections Compendium*, or in a book. For details on doing this, contact ACA's Publications Department at 1-800-222-5646, ext. 1894 or visit our website at www.aca.org.

Jim Gondles

James A. Gondles, Jr., CAE
Executive Director
American Correctional Association

Chapter 1

Introduction and Background

This work is an implementation guide to help administrators and staff handle the youths who are incarcerated in adult facilities. Youths are different from adults, and to manage a prison with regard for the safety of inmates—juveniles and adults—and with concern for staff safety, it is vital to pay special attention to the youths. Such attention will help avoid staff burnout and resignations and lead to a greater potential for rehabilitation of the youths or at least less troublesome behavior from them.

The purpose of this book is to provide the field with a blueprint for action, a road map on how to accomplish the directive of serving youthful offenders in adult correctional systems. The debate is over in many jurisdictions. There is no need to discuss whether young people should be incarcerated in adult institutions, or whether they should serve long sentences according to adult guidelines. Policy makers, legislators, and the public have determined that youths are to be treated as adults and punished for their crimes. As such, we in the profession must provide the most effective and efficient service for this population.

In our prior book, *No Time to Play: Youthful Offenders in Adult Correctional Systems* (1998), we attempted to identify the issues that the justice system faced, as policy makers directed that young people under the age of criminal responsibility (usually sixteen or seventeen years) be tried and sentenced as adults. In that work, we surveyed the correctional systems in North America and reported the major trends and issues our profession faced. We found the following:

- An increased number of juveniles were committing violent offenses, which lawmakers decided required a more severe form of adjudication.
- An increased number of juveniles were redefined as adults through a formal adjudication process in the United States.
- An increasing number of juveniles committed crimes that traditionally had been associated with adults, undermining the traditional juvenile delinquency paradigm.
- An increased number of juveniles were transferred and remanded to adult jurisdictions and facilities.
- Younger juveniles increasingly were being remanded to adult facilities.
- Juveniles committed more violent offenses against persons.
- Young African-American men and women disproportionately were transferred to adult jurisdictions and remanded to adult facilities.
- Young offenders' safety in adult facilities was one of the major problems challenging officials in adult facilities.
- There did not seem to be a systemic effort to develop relevant programs for remanded youthful offenders in adult systems.

- Youthful offenders housed in adult corrections systems will develop more social, emotional, and interpersonal problems, leading to a more vicious hybrid inmate.
- Youthful offenders were labeled by risk and adjudication protocols in an exaggerated fashion beyond the scope of their original criminal behavior.

These fundamental themes continue today. Yet, administrators and other staff can make a difference in the lives of the juveniles in their facilities, and by doing so, can have safer and more humane facilities. This will require thinking about this group of inmates as distinct from the other inmates. The systems that are doing so now (Glick and Rhine, 2001) have turned around many of these so-called intractable youths. The reasons for establishing such programs are varied, but by establishing youthful offender programs, it may be possible to make a change in the recidivism rate of this group and avoid having the juveniles become scarier adult inmates as they age. The number of juveniles who will be coming into adult facilities is expected to increase due to some of the reasons described next. This means that even if you do not presently have a large number of juveniles, in the near future, you are likely to have such a group. It is wise to be prepared for them so that your actions can be proactive rather than reactive.

National Crime Statistics

Many of the youths in correctional facilities have committed violent crime. According to the FBI's *Uniform Crime Reports* (1997), while the rate of murders and violent crimes has decreased among juveniles, the proportion of violent crime continues to rise. Yet, the Bureau of Justice Statistics reported that homicide rates for teenagers between fourteen- and seventeen-years old steadily declined between 1993 and 1998 (2000, p. 2). Also, an estimated 109,800 cases of violent crime (including criminal homicide, forcible rape, robbery, and aggravated assault) were processed in U.S. juvenile courts in 1997. This represents a 15 percent decrease from 1996 (Office of Juvenile Justice and Delinquency Prevention, 2000, Table 1, p. 5).

The Bureau of Justice Statistics compared data collected from the 1989 and 1995 School Crime Supplement to the National Crime Victimization Survey (Puzzanchera, 2000). In comparing the two years' data, the Bureau of Justice Statistics reported (1998, Table 1, pp. 13-14) the presence of street gangs and gang activity in schools nearly doubled during that time period from 15.3 percent to 28.4 percent (Table 4, pg. 19). Drugs continued to be a problem. The availability of drugs, such as marijuana, cocaine, crack, or uppers and downers, increased only slightly. However, the rate was already at 63.2 percent in 1989; that is, 63.2 percent of the students surveyed stated that these drugs were readily available in school (Table 2, pp. 15-16). In addition, there was little or no change in the percentage of students who reported any violent or property victimization at school (Table 1, pp. 13-14).

Also, almost no students reported taking a gun to school (less than .5 percent). Yet, 5.3 percent reported seeing another student with a gun, and 12.7 percent reported knowing another student who brought a gun to school (some 1995 survey questions were not asked in the 1989 study).

To appreciate the magnitude of the youthful offender issues for the adult correctional system, one need only review juvenile corrections data. In 1997, an estimated 1,717,900 delinquency cases (involving juveniles up to seventeen years old) were heard in juvenile courts (Stahl et al., 2000). While this was a slight decrease from the number of cases heard in 1996, the number of juvenile cases administered by juvenile courts had increased 45 percent between 1986 and 1995. This included a 98 percent increase involving offenses against persons, a 23 percent increase in offenses against property, and a 120 percent increase in drug law violations.

These increases are proportionately represented throughout the entire juvenile justice system, including detention, intake diversions, waivers to criminal court, and adjudication. Of particular interest is the waiver to criminal court. In 1997, an estimated 7,800 delinquency cases (involving juveniles up to seventeen years old) were waived; this was down from approximately 9,300 waived cases in 1996 (National Center for Juvenile Justice, 2001). Even though waivers had increased 26 percent between 1988 and 1997, the number of cases waived in 1997 was 16 percent less than in 1996. Of those cases waived in 1997, 40 percent were offenses against persons; 37 percent involved a property offense; and 15 percent involved a drug law violation.

Juvenile vandalism represents a particular problem for the justice systems, since it is one of the more common offenses heard in courts. Indeed, in 1997, an estimated 114,800 cases were processed by juvenile courts (Office of Juvenile Justice and Delinquency Prevention, 2000, Table 1, p. 5). This represents a 41 percent increase in vandalism cases perpetrated by juveniles between 1988 and 1997. In 1997, approximately 841,000 cases involving all forms of property offenses were referred to juvenile courts. Of those cases, 53 percent were handled formally (up from 45 percent in 1988) and 1 percent were waived. Of those property offenses that were nonadjudicated, 23 percent were waived (Office of Juvenile Justice and Delinquency Prevention, 2000, Figure 3, p. 10).

This increase in the proportion of cases being handled formally, combined with an increase in the volume of vandalism cases referred to the courts, resulted in a 54 percent increase in the number of cases handled formally by the courts between 1991 and 1995.

These data are comparable with other offense increases and reflect the get-tough-on-crime policy adopted, de facto, by many jurisdictions within the United States.

Of those juveniles transferred, most represented violent felony offenders with 66 percent charged with a violent offense (11 percent with murder, 34 percent with robbery, and 15 percent with felony assault). As we have reported elsewhere (Glick and Sturgeon, 1998), 63 percent transferred were African-American males. Females continue to represent less than 3 percent of the cases transferred to adult courts. Of the felony cases transferred in 1994, 59 percent were convicted as charged, and 52 percent of those convicted of a felony were sentenced to prison. The average prison sentence for a juvenile convicted in adult court was nine years, with about 33 percent sentenced to less than four years. The average prison sentence for a juvenile convicted of a violent offense was about eleven years. This means that most of the juveniles will be in their mid-to-late twenties when released. They will have become adults while incarcerated.

In the same Bureau of Justice Statistics report, 2 percent of juveniles fifteen or older formally handled in juvenile courts were transferred to criminal courts by judicial waiver. This is similar to what we reported in 1998 (Glick and Sturgeon, pps. 24, 40-41). Thirty-seven percent of the murder cases referred to juvenile court were judicially waived to adult criminal court. Of the juveniles processed in juvenile court, 48 percent were Caucasian males; 36 percent were African-American males; 7 percent were Caucasian females; and 5 percent were African-American females. Fifty-five percent were actually adjudicated delinquent, and among those adjudicated, 40 percent received residential placement, and 50 percent received formal probation.

Gangs and Gang Behavior

It is important to understand the dynamics of gang activity and the influence it has on juvenile crime. In fact, gang behavior has tremendous impact on the gang activity that occurs within the American prison system. As such, we highlight several critical factors as an introduction to this most important area. In later chapters, we discuss how to manage gang behavior of violent youth within the adult corrections system. A useful resource in this area is *Gangbusters: Strategies for Prevention and Intervention* by Lonnie Jackson (1988), which may serve as part of a model program that can be adapted for adult facilities.

The first national gang survey was conducted by the National Youth Gang Center (1997), which collected information from local law enforcement agencies throughout the United States. A total of 1,216 police departments serving large cities (with populations over 25,000) were surveyed. Another 664 suburban-county police and sheriff's departments were also queried. A random sampling of rural police and sheriff's departments also were invited to provide information about gang activities.

The results of the survey indicated that the youth gang problem in this country affects communities of all sizes, in urban, suburban, and rural areas, and its impact is substantial. Seventy-five percent of large urban cities reported that they had youth gang activity. The demographic attributes of gang members are changing. However, African-Americans and Latinos continue to comprise the majority of U.S. gang members. Approximately 33 percent of gang members in rural and small counties were Caucasian. Further, it was reported that gang members were involved in significant amounts of crime, although the type and severity of the criminal activity varied by the type of locality. According to the following year's survey, an estimated 780,200 gang members formed 28,700 youth gangs in 4,463 jurisdictions across the country in 1998 (Office of Juvenile Justice and Delinquency Prevention, 2000).

Gang activity also has increased within schools. As a result of the number of violent incidents at schools that occurred during the 1997-1998 academic year, President Clinton challenged the Departments of Education and Justice to produce an annual report on school violence, with recommendations for school safety. *The Annual Report on School Safety* (1998) indicated that between 1989 and 1995, the percentage of students who reported that street gangs were present in their schools increased by 13 percent (from 15 percent in 1989 to 28 percent in 1995).

The Office of Juvenile Justice and Delinquency Prevention long has been a proponent of research and programs for gang intervention and suppression. They have devoted years of time and money to the study and program design for gang prevention and intervention. Two longitudinal studies supported by the Office of Juvenile Justice and Delinquency Prevention (1998) in juvenile gang research were those in Seattle, Washington, and Rochester, New York.

The fundamental question posed in each of these studies was: Does gang membership contribute to delinquency above and beyond the influence of associating with delinquent peers? In Rochester, New York and Seattle, Washington, results indicated that it does. Gang membership was associated with increased participation in substance abuse and delinquency. This was true even when gang youth were compared with youth who associated with delinquent peers.

Stahl posited that according to interactional theory, delinquency is caused by the patterns of interactions between individuals and their environment. As bonds to parents and teachers (conventional social roles and relationships) weaken, social control is reduced and criminality becomes more probable. These issues become critically important and instructive, especially as we begin to attempt to manage the youthful offenders in our adult correctional systems.

Amnesty International's Findings

Amnesty International (1998) published a scathing report: *Betraying the Young: Human Rights Violations Against Children in the United States Justice System*, detailing human rights violations perpetrated against children who are in the U.S. justice systems. While administrators may not be able to do anything about the policy questions, they can note the problem areas and suggest solutions to policy makers to reduce some of the reported abuses. Then, they can share their successes so that others can learn from what they have done. *See*, for example, Glick and Rhine, *Journal of Correctional Best Practices: Juveniles in Adult Correctional Systems* (2001).

Additionally, they can structure programs for youthful offenders that rely on standards issued by the American Correctional Association. They also can follow some of the suggestions in this work, especially in regard to providing training for those who will work with youthful offenders, and can provide monitoring of conditions by administrators at all levels. Other concerns that can be targeted include providing sufficient mental health resources and training for staff on issues of mental health concerns so they learn when to intervene, when and how to use restraints, and the proper and improper uses of solitary confinement.

Many detained youth are mentally ill or suffer from severe emotional disturbances. Sometimes confinement adds to their disturbance. Therefore, facilities must screen minors for mental health problems, provide emergency psychological services, establish procedures for dealing with suicidal youngsters, make sure that medications are prescribed and administered by qualified medical personnel, establish provisions for children to request psychological care, and make sure that there is adequate staff for ongoing psychological services

(Austin, Johnson, and Gregoriou, 2000).

Discrimination within the Justice System Towards Children

Children are considered those individuals under the age of eighteen. The Amnesty International report establishes criterion for its conclusions and recommendations based on two primary sources. First, there are international human rights standards such as treaties ratified by the United States and other United Nations' Resolutions and Rules and U.S. laws and standards promulgated by nongovernmental bodies, including the American Correctional Association. While the report cites the United States as making a significant contribution to the development of the international system of human rights protection throughout the twentieth century, it does admonish the United States for its resistance to the international commitments it has made, and others it has failed to keep. This includes

The Convention on the Rights of the Child that has been ratified by 192 United Nations' members, all except the United States and Somalia.

Second, the report cites U.S. laws and standards as defined in federal, state, and municipal statutes and codes. A corollary source are those standards promulgated by "nongovernmental" bodies. The report specifically mentions the American Correctional Association as an organization that sets standards and guidelines for the treatment of offenders in correctional systems.

The Use of Force and Restraints

The Human Rights Division of the U.S. Department of Justice has aggressively pursued civil rights violations of children and youths incarcerated in both the juvenile and adult justice systems. Reports contend that staff in institutions have physically abused children and youths under their care. Amnesty states that children have been punched, kicked, shackled, hog-tied, sprayed with chemicals, and even shocked with cattle prods. Since then, several of the states mentioned in the *Amnesty* report have been developing better programs for their juveniles. The authors have served as consultants for several of them. Yet, much more needs to be done.

The reasons for the abuse of force and allegations about restraints often are cited as the result of inadequate staff training in working with the youth population, crowding, inadequate numbers of staff on duty, high turnover of staff, and inadequate monitoring and accountability. The bulk of this work will examine each of these concerns and present some alternatives so that the future does not have to replicate the past.

Solitary Confinement

Public correctional policy allows for solitary confinement of children and youths when they present an imminent danger to themselves or others, and/or when less restrictive methods of behavior control have been applied and failed. However, the National Juvenile Detention Association position statement on conditions of confinement (Parent et al., 1994) calculated that in 1992 there had been 435,000 occasions when facilities had used isolation for a period of 1 to 24 hours. It further reported that there were 88,900 occasions when it had been imposed for more than 24 hours. In many institutions, children and youths had been confined without access to services and exercise. How does your jurisdiction fare on this dimension? Do you have a policy on the use of solitary confinement? Does the staff know what it is? Is it followed?

Inadequate Services for Youthful Offenders with Mental Health Problems

Amnesty International cites two concerns that inhibit adequate mental health services for youths incarcerated in juvenile corrections systems, and this often may be true of youths in adult systems, as well. The first is the lack of mental health services that cause children to be deposited into justice systems rather than remaining in the community. The second is the lack of mental health services within both the adult and juvenile justice systems. This includes inadequately trained staff to diagnose mental health problems, and inappropriate staff intervention. Staff may be using restraints improperly, or inappropriately using force or solitary confinement. Again, the Human Rights Division of the Department of Justice has taken a special interest in this area and aggressively has pursued inadequate systems and allegations of inadequacy. As a result, Georgia, Louisiana, and Puerto Rico are proactively reinventing their juvenile justice systems.

Concerns about Juveniles in the Adult Justice System

Amnesty International expressed concerns about children in five areas of the adult justice system, and it is important to review these areas so readers can assess their own systems. These areas included:

- **Failure to separate children from adults.** Adult prisons are unsafe places for juveniles. Juveniles in prison continue to be targets of physical abuse from older inmates and/or staff. They continue to be victims of sexual abuse and assaults. While this condition is widely known and acknowledged, and there are international and national standards that advocate separation of juveniles from adult inmate populations, the application of these regulations is inconsistent at best, and deliberately ignored at worst. The separation issue is further compounded by inconsistent application of the standards by policy makers and corrections authorities. For example, in 1974 the U.S. Congress legislated financial incentives to states that separate children from adult inmates (Juvenile Justice Prevention Act).

However by 1998, that U.S. Congress adopted legislation permitting regulatory changes and relaxing the "separation of juveniles from adults" requirement for states. As a result of public hearings, the government took the position that it would be prudent to allow individual states to decide the circumstances under which a juvenile could or should be housed with adults. Indeed, in a 1997-1998 Amnesty International survey of state adult correctional systems (Table 1, Report Appendix), 40 states reported housing children in the general population, with more than 3,700 children in custody. Then, 12 states reported that they house children with inmates aged up to 21, and there were approximately 2,000 juveniles in that situation. Additionally, most of the states that house children with adults reported that they do not provide special programs for young prisoners. The situation is more severe for young women and girls. In jails, the situation is worse (Austin, Johnson, and Gregoriou, 2000).

- **Harsh, inflexible sentences.** The Amnesty International Report admonishes U.S. policy for being too rigid when imposing sentences on children who have been sentenced as adults. Indeed, the adult penal code often requires minimum sentences to be imposed for certain crimes that are committed. We have detailed this issue in our own work (Glick and Sturgeon, 1998; Glick and Goldstein, 1995) and found that young offenders proportionately spend a greater proportion of their lives imprisoned for the very same crime committed by their adult counterparts. Additionally, life without parole is both quantitatively and qualitatively very different for a juvenile (even one who is seventeen or eighteen) than it is for one who is thirty. In our own visits to adult institutions serving juveniles, we have met and interviewed young offenders who will serve forty and fifty years in prison as a result of their crimes. Some of these crimes are not violent felonies, but rather drug crimes that carry harsh sentences. Corrections administrators and managers will have to program creatively for these youthful offenders, who will spend more time in prison than a first-year correctional officer will spend in the same system before retiring.
- **Failure to specify a minimum age of criminal responsibility.** While administrators cannot do anything about the age of those who come to prison, they can be prepared for the youthful offenders who will be arriving, and perhaps suggest to policy makers why there should be changes.
- **Length of time before trial.** Again, on this issue, administrators may not be able to make changes in their system but they can inform policy makers of the genuine concerns in this area so that changes can be initiated. The Sixth Amendment to the U.S. Constitution guarantees a speedy trial to all citizens. In part, the amendment states:

In all criminal prosecutions, the accused shall enjoy the right to a speedy and public trial, by an impartial jury of the State and district wherein the crime shall have been committed, which district shall have been previously ascertained by law, and to be informed of the nature and cause of the accusation; to be confronted with the witnesses against him; to have compulsory process for obtaining witnesses in his favor, and to have the assistance of counsel for his defense.

Studies have shown that between six and nine months is the average waiting time for individuals arrested and awaiting trial (Brown and Langan, 1994; Butts and Halemba,

1994). While juvenile cases may receive some preferential treatment, juveniles often spend long periods of time in detention facilities, many of which are not prepared to provide programs for them. Georgia Juvenile Court Judge, the Honorable Glenda Hutchett, stated in a 1968 court hearing:

When we place children in institutions where they often sit for months, accused but not convicted, we lose a window of opportunity to turn their lives around. We do nothing more than create better criminals. These children inevitably reenter society no better equipped to be productive citizens than when they were first detained. Automatically trying children as adults gives up on them before we have made any real effort to show them a better way (Commission on Corrections Court Review, 1969).

- **Lack of access to education and other services.** Administrators can do something about this concern. The Amnesty International Report corroborated what had been reported by the Department of Justice, Office of Human Rights. Many prisons have failed to provide adequate education programs, special needs programs, and critical developmental services to children and youths incarcerated within their jurisdictions. Indeed, we have suggested that youthful offenders in adult corrections systems were inadequately served in important developmental programs such as education, counseling, mental health services, and medical services (Glick and Sturgeon, 1998). Amnesty International staff visited jails and prisons throughout the United States, interviewed many youthful inmates, and determined that education, health, and mental health services were inadequate or nonexistent in both the juvenile and adult systems. (*See also* U.S. Department of Health and Human Services, *Mental Health: A Report of the Surgeon General* (1999)).

Unfortunately, the adult criminal justice systems are not subject to the same statutes and regulations as youth-serving institutions, and in many cases, they ignore the developmental need of the youths placed in their care. Until the summer of 1998, when Congress reauthorized the Individual Disability Education Act (IDEA), special education services were not required to be provided to youths if they were incarcerated in adult correctional systems. The amended law now requires such services to be provided to all inmates in adult systems if they have been certified by special education committees, and they must be provided the required education services as if these offenders were in regular public school.

Juveniles in Adult Prisons and Jails: A National Assessment (Austin, Johnson, Gregoriou, 2000) indicated that between 42 and 60 percent of the juvenile populations incarcerated in Arizona, Florida, and Maine are classified as special education. These high percentages probably are typical of the youth who are incarcerated as adults. We need to insure that special education services are provided if we are to adequately habilitate the juveniles in our correctional systems. To the degree possible, correctional educators should identify those youthful offenders in need of special education services and provide it to them. Such intervention will assist in the transition of those offenders when it comes time to either transfer them to the general population within the prison, or as they return to their communities.

Summary

The violence among young people in our communities and schools has led to greater intolerance on the part of the average citizen toward young offenders. As such, even more states have chosen to treat young people as adults, sentencing them to longer periods of incarceration, at even younger ages. Indeed, as we have traveled throughout the country visiting adult systems, we have observed younger children incarcerated in adult systems for longer periods of time. For example, one female program in the northwest has an offender serving a fifty-one-year sentence, another a forty-year sentence, and a third serving twenty-seven years. While each now is maintained in a young offender program within an adult prison, they will have to transfer to an adult population when they reach their eighteenth birthday.

The implementation of programs and services for youthful offenders in adult systems becomes even more crucial to adult correctional operations as we continue on this pathway of more harsh treatment of young offenders who have committed violent crimes against persons or property. Yet, administrators and staff can make a difference in the lives of these youthful offenders, and as a result, in the efficient operation of the facility.

There continues to be debate about the most appropriate intervention for these young offenders who are placed in adult systems. The conservative policy maker continues to demand harsh punishment regardless of offender age, with little or no concern for the young person who ultimately will be released into the very community for which we seek relief and protection. The public advocate who is concerned for incarcerated youth shadows the operations of the corrections systems, thus insuring zero tolerance for abuse; insuring there are programs for the mentally ill and special needs offender; and litigating whenever standards fall below expectations. Corrections professionals continue to debate the merits of habilitation and treatment versus safety and control, often yielding to political pressures and community lobbyists.

In other words, youthful offenders are already in the midst of adult correctional systems, without many things—without adequate policy direction or adequate age-appropriate programs and services, without competent staff trained to deal with normal adolescent growth and development, and lacking an infrastructure and support system to insure the health and safety of staff and offenders, whether they be incarcerated or in the community.

No Time to Play (1998) provides many suggestions on how to deal with the most critical issues of placing young offenders in adult systems. In this area, administrators and staff can make a difference. Some of their roles include policy formulation and direction; program development, design, and implementation; staff training and development; programming for special needs populations; and program administration and operations.

Concerns of the Chief Executive

Many chief executive officers within the profession continue to ponder:

- What is the best mechanism by which to identify and create policy direction?
- How does a chief executive officer help the organization make a transition to better serve the youth population?
- What mandates and agency procedures should be promulgated to insure health and safety?
- Even if a system endorses adolescent development as critical to young offender program operations, how are these concepts translated and applied in a practical way?
- What is the best organizational structure and management system to use with this population?
- How is staff developed and trained, in accordance with current paradigms and experience?
- What are the budget requirements, and given no additional resources, what priorities should be established?
- What is the best system to manage youth behavior appropriately?
- What kinds of tools are available to monitor programs and manage implementation?
- What planning process is required to implement policy direction and manage operations for these youthful offenders?

We begin our exploration of this issue with an overview of the conceptual framework that was first described in *No Time to Play* (1998). In this first chapter, we reviewed the relevant concepts of treating and programming for youthful offenders in adult correctional systems. We reviewed some of the issues that have been raised by policy makers, governmental agencies, and advocacy groups. In Chapter 2, we introduce a strategy for planning a youthful offender program within an adult corrections system. The information here will provide the reader with functional planning skills. Through a series of tactics, charts, and tables, we provide a functional planning strategy that is focused and easy to adopt, whether the system is a large jurisdiction or smaller one, such as an institution within a system. Chapter 3 provides nuts and bolts, hands-on information on how to operate a youthful offender program within an adult correctional system.

Our no-nonsense approach provides frameworks for action, which easily may be adapted and used in any system. In Chapter 4, we provide the how to's and what if's in program implementation. In this chapter, we provide forms, letters, and the actual materials to get the program operational. As we see the trends and themes involved in this complex area of youths who commit crimes, we may begin to appreciate the magnitude of the challenge as we receive these youthful offenders into our adult systems. We end our work with a look at where we have been and then examine the future, including the applications of what we have learned thus far, and what we yet must discover.

Chapter 2

Planning:

Getting from Here to There

Introduction

There is no debate, no more discussion, and no more positions for which to advocate. Young people who commit violent crimes, or participate in criminal activity that jeopardizes property or persons, creating unsafe community conditions by their actions, often will be tried and sentenced as adults. These young people will spend a long period of time incarcerated in adult justice systems. It is no longer a question whether young persons under the legal age of responsibility (sixteen in some states, eighteen in most states) should be tried and sentenced as adults. Rather, the questions are as follows: **Now that these youthful offenders are placed in adult systems, what do we do with them? How do we manage their behaviors? And how do we insure their safety and security?**

Perhaps one of the more important, crucial tasks a staff must perform is planning. Yet, the one administrative function most ignored within the justice systems by a majority of its staff is that of planning. Casey Stengel (one of the great baseball managers) said, "If you don't know where you are going, you'll end up somewhere else." Indeed, most correctional systems seem to be "going somewhere else." In some cases, some correctional systems "end up somewhere else" even when they know where they are going, simply because they do not know how to get where they want to be.

Unfortunately, many correctional system staff do not have planning skills specifically needed to design programs for youthful offenders, nor has it been a priority for them. They simply are not trained to effectively identify problems associated with youthful offender populations, evaluate causes, identify system effects, establish normative goals, define observable and measurable objectives, and, finally, identify a range of possible strategies necessary to make an enlightened decision. Even when these tasks are done for them, the typical correctional staff member often is either unable, unwilling or does not know how to implement tactics to achieve what has been identified. However, with positive leadership from the top, this can be changed.

The purpose of this chapter is to identify a functional planning process that may be adapted for any correctional system, no matter how large or small. It does not matter if the system is a large state agency, an institution, or a small community-based program. A planning process is one that may be used in any of these domains because it is the function that directs what needs to be accomplished, not the structure of the organization itself.

However, the planning process must be directed and administered by the highest administrative level within the organization. Yes, even the secretary of a large state mega-agency, the commissioner of a department, the director of an office, the warden of an institution, the supervisor of a unit, the correctional officer responsible for the cell block—all of these, at every level of management, must know what it means to perform a planning process.

They must be well-versed in using a planning process as a management and administrative tool, and they must be prepared to supervise the development, design, and implementation of a planning function. Jurisdictions such as Alaska, Colorado, Louisiana, Nevada, South Carolina, and Washington have used this approach successfully to design their own youthful offender systems (Glick and Rhine, 2001; Glick and Sturgeon, 1998).

Planning Pays

Every correctional program, including those for youthful offenders, has stakeholders, those individuals or entities who have a vested interest in what is happening with the program. For the private sector, it may be the stockholders, the funders, or the board of directors. For the public sector, it may be the legislature, the governor's office, or the citizens themselves. As such, the planning process and the eventual plan that is produced provides the stakeholders with a shared vision. The manager uses this plan to give the stakeholders their own vibrant, reflective, targeted, and attainable vision of the future.

Stakeholders also have a vested interest in the success of the program. Therefore, the plan should provide them with an understanding of how the manager sees their involvement and the future of the organization—including their role. The plan also provides stakeholders with accurate, precise information about the organization that they support. In other words, the plan is a written document that provides information to those who must support the program with their energy, efforts, resources, and position power.

There are other reasons to insure the youthful offender program has a well-articulated plan. The plan and the planning process does the following things:

- provides **accountability**, in that it insures well-defined accomplishments and shows how funds are expended to achieve stated objectives
- insures that an **evaluation** is conducted, since the plan articulates standards for staff and program outcomes
- facilitates **organizational management** because the planning document will detail tactical implementation of *what* is done, *when*, by *whom*, and *how*
- directs and focuses **goal-attainment** activities
- reduces **crisis management** and reaction to operational issues by increasing proactive interventions and deliberate administrative actions
- improves **coordination** among and between departments, and between the system and its stakeholders
- maximizes **limited resources** and **funds** by directing planned interventions and strategies
- improves **public and community relations**

- improves **staff morale** by publishing the mission, goals, objectives, and interventions of the organization for all to implement and monitor
- motivates **staff** and **volunteers** into positive action

Without planning, things can be random, and randomness in a prison is a recipe for disaster.

What is Planning?

Planning is a process that produces a product. We shall focus on two planning products, both blueprints that direct and focus action. The first is a management plan that articulates the connection between a jurisdiction's mission and its programs and services. The second is an implementation plan, which specifically describes how the jurisdiction will insure that its mission, goals, objectives, and strategies will be accomplished. We shall elaborate on each of these in a bit, but first let us examine the process of planning. Just how do we engage an entire organization in a systemic course of action that leads to a coherent planning document that all may use as a tool for success?

Responsibility Charting

A fundamental principle for successful plan development requires that all members of an organization be involved in the planning process. No matter what their title, level of responsibility, span of control, or position of authority, all staff must have input into the process and take responsibility for the product that is developed. Anything less makes the process ineffective, and the product will be a less-than-useful tool for policy implementation and organizational administration.

Planning requires collaborative relations among many different components of the organization, and an equal number of different individuals within units of the organization. Decisions within the planning process transect lines of authority, often requiring mangers and their staff from different organizational levels and structures to participate in plan development. It is critically important for the planning process to provide a mechanism to divide these responsibilities among the various roles and relationships of the stakeholders to insure that the most efficient planning process is accomplished.

One such method is "responsibility charting" (Gilmore and Nelson, 1978). This is based on the principles of complex organizations that Galbraith (1973) discussed and that Melcher (1967) assessesed as he studied roles and relationships within these organizations.

Responsibility charting is a technique that is indifferent to the lines and levels of authority within the organizational unit. Using this technique, individuals are assigned responsibility for situations, problems, or issues regardless of their position, role, or function within the organization. The key to using responsibility charting as a planning tool depends on first understanding that responsibility for any given task or planning process varies, and there are degrees of one's responsibility for and involvement in a particular task or planning function. For our purposes, the degrees of responsibility may be defined in four ways.

(R) **Responsible.** This is the person who takes the initiative in the particular area, develops the alternatives, analyzes the situation, and makes an initial recommendation.

(A) **Approve.** This is the person who either signs off or vetoes a decision before it becomes effective, or who chooses from alternatives developed by the "R" role.

(C) **Consult.** This is a person who is consulted prior to a decision being made, but who has no veto power on the issue.

(I) **Inform.** This is a person who must be notified after a decision, but who need not be consulted prior to a decision being made.

Chart 2.1 — Sample Matrix for Decision Making

Units / Decisions	Warden	Deputy Warden	Security Chief	Program Director
Design Cell Block	I	A	R	C
Identify Youth Population	I	A	C	R
Design Program	I	A	C	R
Initiate Service	A	C	I	I

A Matrix for Decision Making

Once the individuals in a system understand and accept that responsibility for planning may be shared throughout the entire organization, it does not matter what level of authority or role one plays in the system. Then, a matrix (*see* Chart 2.1) may be developed for each area of the plan. Individuals who are involved with the particular planning area are placed across the top of the matrix, and the decision, product, or activities are placed down the left margin. In each cell that is formed by the individual and the activity, a responsibility code letter is entered. This is derived as a result of consensus among the planning group. Note that the warden, who is traditionally perceived as the ultimate decision maker, is responsible for none of the activities listed, approves only one of the activities, and for three of the activities, is informed after a decision is approved. This is often the case when responsibility charting is used in decision making and planning. In effect, it frees the chief executive officer and other staff to manage their systems and administer the policies with greater efficiency and integrity.

The steps to implement responsibility charting are easy and straightforward. They include the following items:

1. Identify the specific planning areas that need to be articulated or decisions that must be made.
2. List all of the individuals who should participate in the identified planning area or decision point.
3. Combine the participants and decisions or planning activities to form a chart similar to Chart 2.1.
4. Assign the responsibility levels in each of the cells. Be sure to place an "X" in the cells for individuals who may have no involvement with the planning area, so that every cell of the chart is complete.
5. Have the group members resolve any discrepancies or gaps in the chart, sharing responsibilities between members or units, if necessary.
6. Schedule follow-up meetings, as necessary, to monitor implementation.

Potential Problems

While there are many advantages to using responsibility charting, there are inherent problems with the process if one is not careful in its correct application. For example, if one participant becomes involved as the primary individual responsible across all of the planning actions or decision points, the group has allowed **excessive vertical charting.** The individuals involved in the planning process should inquire whether this is a proper use of the individual's time, and if the final task can be done without undue work on one person's part, or whether it would be better to split it among a few members of the group.

Excessive horizontal charting is when most of the planning participants choose to get involved in selected areas of the plan, taking initiative or responsibility for one of the activities to the exclusion of the others. Key individuals, in effect, may not become involved sufficiently or effectively with all of the planning area activities to insure the final product will be accomplished. As such, difficult or tedious tasks may be inadvertently or deliberately overlooked.

Yet, a third potential problem area for this planning technique occurs when the participants cannot reach a **consensus** about their respective roles. Participants either may disagree about who is to do what, or misunderstand the terms of their responsibility assignments. In such cases, not understanding key roles and responsibilities detracts from the obligations participants need to have to insure the process is successful. A corollary pitfall to this problem area is the propensity for the group to defer to the chain of command for decision making. It is essential that the managers and administrators involved in this process guard against the pressure to assume responsibility either for decision making or the planning process.

Management Plans

Management plans are just what the title suggests—documents that articulate the process of how the system delivers its programs and services. Management planning for youthful offenders focuses on how these services are provided to youthful offenders and whether they are institutionalized or in their communities. The planning process that produces a management plan for youthful offenders is constant across systems and rarely needs to be modified because of system functions. That is, institutional and community-based personnel employ the same process to produce a management plan, which lends itself to cross-systems planning. Chart 2.2 depicts the management planning process.

Chart 2.2 The Management Planning Process

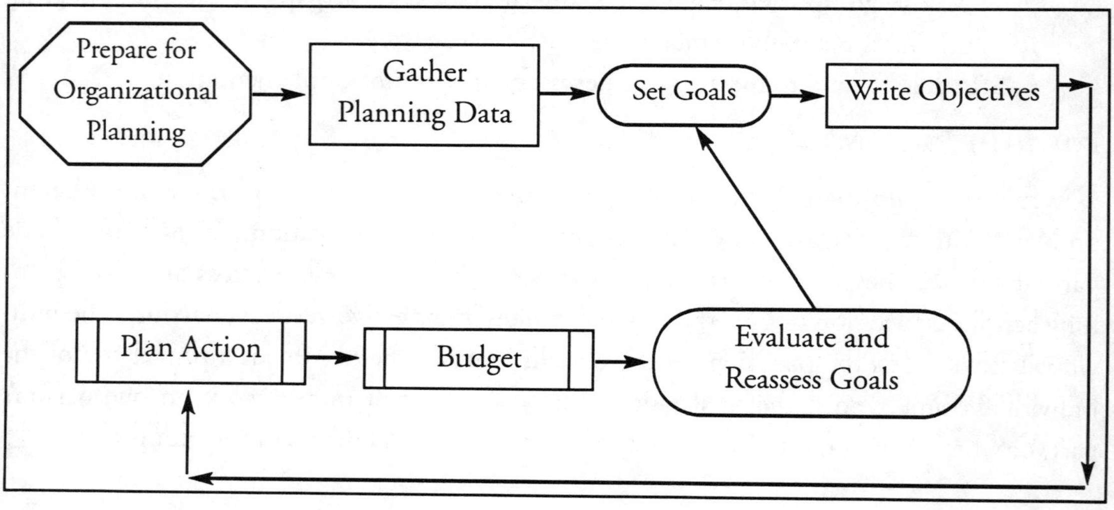

Step One: Readying the system to develop a management plan requires that the whole system must be prepared to work cohesively as a team to produce a product that it is willing to implement. As such, a number of critical areas must be addressed:

Organizational Climate. Such issues as policy and administrative procedures, supervisory relationships, work conditions, salary, peer relationships, status, work conditions, and safety and security, need to be adequate and inventoried. The organizational climate can be assessed either formally by using any of the commercially available tools such as the Moos Work Environmental Scale; or it may be assessed informally by developing a survey that can be completed by the work force. If an informal survey is used, be sure that all the areas of the organizational climate are included, such as organization and policies; the staff job function; supervision; and peer relationships.

Productive Meetings. The planning process relies on effective and efficient communication within an organization, and staff meetings should reflect the mission, goals, and objectives of the system. The planning group must have a facilitator who acts as the group leader, and whose role it is to keep the meeting focused and on task. As such, the facilitator must be proficient in group process rather than just the content area. The facilitator should direct the group in brainstorming, using problem-solving techniques, ensuring that ideas and opinions are expressed freely, recording statements on chart paper, and publishing meeting notes.

The facilitator also should be keenly aware of the physical design of the meeting room. Planning sessions require critical thinking, and this requires a great deal of energy from all who participate. Therefore, it is critically important that the room be well lit, adequately ventilated, and furnished with water (or other refreshments). Some room set-ups are more conducive to the planning function than others. The following are the more typical:

The Lecture Hall or Classroom—The focus is on the group leader to supply most, if not all, of the information for participants. This is probably the least desirable physical plan design for a planning meeting.

The Semicircle—This is a very good set-up for high-participation planning process meetings. All participants can see each other easily, and at the same time, they can see the facilitator and easel for reference to discussion points.

Round Table (Circle)—This is also a good design to encourage discussion among group members. However, some of the group may have their backs to the group facilitator and easel. As such, the facilitator must insure that all members of the group can see and hear what is occurring, so the facilitator should walk about making eye contact with all the group members.

Square Table (Rectangle)—This configuration also works well for small groups. However, those with the most authority, within the organization tend to sit at the ends of the table, thereby potentially discouraging participation and open discussion.

Horseshoe—This physical plant design works well with medium-sized groups and encourages group participation and discussion. The format lends itself well to groups that must take notes and/or refer to written materials.

Several Round Tables—This configuration is best for large group meetings that require participation. As such, the planning process and discussion may be encouraged at each of the tables. Since an informal, participatory atmosphere is engendered, each table, as a subgroup, may be encouraged to report their deliberations.

Planning Process List

Once you have insured that the physical plant is conducive to your planning activities, you can employ several methods to insure the most productive meeting is conducted. The following are a series of items that must be addressed to aid you in the management planning process and the development of a product:

1. Appoint an impartial facilitator as leader of the group.
2. Appoint a person as group recorder who will publish the important statements of participants on chart paper, and who will write minutes of the meeting. Do not rely on the group's history or memory.
3. At the outset of the meeting, set an agenda and time limits for each of the items on the agenda.
4. Appoint a timekeeper who will keep the participants within the agenda's time allocations.
5. Frequently summarize and review what the planning meeting participants have discussed and items on which they have agreed.
6. Reflect or mirror back to the group what is happening in the meeting. The process of the group is to constantly check assumptions group members express (explicitly or implicitly).
7. Be positive.
8. Use the responsibility charting method for decision making, consensus building, and planning process deliberations.
9. Consider including an informal time before the meeting for socialization, so participants warm up to each other and may catch up on formal and informal news.
10. Keep the agenda flexible, and make sure all personal agendas are identified before continuing with the meeting.

11. Compliment individuals for completing tasks and publicly acknowledge participants for achieving results.
12. Consider meeting away from the regular workplace to insure focused attention to the planning process and to create a safe meeting environment.
13. Encourage positive confrontation and full discussion of issues to insure quality products and group consensus; yet, remain neutral so as to mediate differences, if necessary.
14. Follow up between planning meetings with subcommittee work so as to manage the work product and avoid potential problems or unproductive subgroups.

Supporting the Planning Process

It is critically important that the management planning process have the support of the policy makers of the system, at the very least. With that as a foundation, management must be prepared to administer the planning process. How does one start the process? After policy has been determined to create a management plan for the system, the entire organization needs to understand the scope and function of the process. One of the first priorities then, is to create a planning committee.

Such a committee needs to be based on the system's organizational structure and management philosophy. A participatory process that engages all sectors of the system is preferable. The committee should have representation from a cross section of the system, from all supervisory levels, representing a variety of roles and functions. The committee members, in turn, are delegated authority for decision making within the planning process and act as a conduit for information and task completion with their respective units.

Chart 2.3: Planning Committee with Links to Organizational Units

X = committee members
△ = organizational units

As Chart 2.3 depicts, each committee member is assigned by a particular organizational unit to represent its position for any given planning issue. In turn, each individual relates the actions of the planning committee back to the unit along with assignments that must be completed. This type of linkage structure allows for the planning process to be equal across organizational units and within the hierarchical chain-of-command structures.

THE MISSION STATEMENT

The mission statement is a concise statement, usually about 100 words or less, of what services or products the organization provides, how they are provided (that is, what activities or technology is used), and who is involved. There are five core elements of a mission statement. First, it is realistic, accurately reflecting the ideal of what the organization would like to accomplish. Second, the mission statement is clear and concise, succinctly stating how the mission will be accomplished.

The third element indicates who the organization serves, keeping in mind that there may be primary and secondary consumers and recipients of services. For example, the primary recipients of the agency mission may be offenders placed by courts with the department of corrections. The secondary recipients may be communities and/or citizens, who must be kept safe from criminal activities. The fourth element reflects the organization's beliefs and attitudes. Finally, a mission statement is powerful. That is, it immediately strikes the reader with a potent assertion of vision and direction.

An example of a mission statement for a youthful offender system is as follows:

> The youthful offender system is a comprehensive model that delivers habilitation programs and services to violent youthful offenders sentenced to the (jurisdiction) department of corrections. We are a community of concerned staff, committed to the principles of adolescent development, who through modeling, mentoring, and using other planned interventions, provide opportunities for youthful offenders to acquire the beliefs, skills, and abilities that will enable them to grow and develop into successful, productive, citizens.

GATHERING DATA

Planning requires knowledge. The planning group should collect information and gather data that informs the planning process before it begins to develop the organization's plan. No matter whether the organization is an institution, or a community-based service, information in key areas needs to be collected and analyzed. Such data sets should include information about the offender who is served, the community's opinion and demographics, the organization and its capability, the organization's mission, and the stakeholders' viewpoints.

Before goals and objectives can be written, there must be a concentrated effort to collect the data that will inform those goals and objectives. What are the needs of the offenders you will serve? Will that population be predominantly special needs? Are they younger offenders, or closer to the age of majority? How do they process knowledge and information? All of these factors become critical as the organizational plan is developed. It ultimately will have an impact on the resources that are needed, the staffing pattern required, and the organizational structure, among other issues.

Community opinion also informs the planning process. The planning group should interview a cross section of the community and include prominent residents, government and civic leaders, school officials, business owners, the faith community, law enforcement, health care, and young people. The planning process is informed and enriched by information gathered from these sectors that are specific to the organization's role within the community, interactions among them, and projects that may be pursued.

The organizational capabilities are critically important to develop a planning product that will be useful as a dynamic tool. Some sort of resource inventory is preferable in order to standardize the collection of data. If the planning group chooses to assess its organization informally, that is, use some survey or locally designed questionnaire, then it is imperative that at least seven core areas be addressed. These include: program leadership; finance and resources; staff competencies and expertise; equipment; facilities; advisory group and stakeholders; and volunteers. In each of these areas, information should be collected about their strengths, weaknesses, and actions needed to overcome impediments.

There are also recently developed and well-validated formal assessments that can help when evaluating the organization. One such instrument is the Correctional Program Assessment Inventory (CPAI) (Gendreau and Andrews, 1994). The CPAI and the CPAI-Revised are based on results from a variety of meta-analysis of correctional effectiveness studies conducted over the last decade and based on the works of Gendreau, Andrews, and Lipsey. Based on empirical data from these and other studies, the CPAI collects information in six core areas:

1. *Program Implementation and Leadership*—The influence and involvement of the program director is measured; leadership qualifications, and implementation and design of the program are examined.
2. *Client Assessment*—The selection of clients, the assessment of specific characteristics, and the process of assessment is reviewed.
3. *Program Characteristics*—The types of treatment used, how they are used, and their ability to target criminogenic needs are investigated.
4. *Staff Characteristics*—Staff education levels and variety of training offered ro the staff, are surveyed; experience, longevity on the job, and details on how staff are assessed are documented.
5. *Evaluation*—The types of program assessments, evaluations, and quality assurance are reviewed.

6. *Miscellaneous*—This includes an assesment of such factors as ethical guidelines for intervention, completion and documentation of client records, details on what and how advisory boards are used, and the type and amount of community support.

The CPAI is a useful assessment tool to collect data about the organization and can be readily scored. It has national normative data, and the organization can be evaluated in reference to others both locally and across the nation.

Setting Goals and Writing Objectives

Goals

Goals are long-range targets that project the hopes of the organization at least five years into the future. Goals move the system closer to its mission, and are intentions of the way the organization would like to be in the future. Goals force the system to stretch beyond its present capacity. Goals should be developed and designed without regard to resources. While this position is contrary to popular expert opinion (most suggest that goals be developed within existing resources), the best designed goals force the organization to stretch its paradigm of operation and go beyond where they currently operate.

Public managers need to deal with three sets of goals. The first set are goals that do not require the expansion of the organization's activity. Goals of this sort allow the organization to remain stagnant. The second set of goals allows the system to expand at a modest rate, that is, a deliberate extension or development of programs and new systems.

Finally, the third set includes goals that enable the organization to maximize its dreams and move toward its mission. These goals are wish statements that seem impractical for the short term, but stimulate the organization to grow, develop, perform, and achieve. The difference between a goal that maintains the status quo and a goal that forces the organization's leap into a five-year action plan may mean the difference between the reduction of recidivism and continued incarceration for the youthful offender. Table 2.1 is a checklist of questions to answer when formulating goals for the organization's planning process. Use the list to develop each goal that is created.

It is necessary to analyze the goals you brainstorm, and place these in priority order. To accomplish this task, we suggest that you use some form of force field analysis technique. There are a variety of formats that can be used as long as there is a systematic way of listing the goals that have been developed, and then identifing those factors that help or impede goal achievement and those strategies that also either strengthen or weaken goal attainment. Table 2.2 is an example of applying force field analytic techniques.

Table 2.1: Questions to Answer When Formulating Goals—A Checklist

#	Questions
1	Where do we want to be in five years? Ten years?
2	What are we doing now that we should not be doing five years from now?
3	What aren't we doing now that we should be doing in five years?
4	How will our client population change in the next five years? How can we keep up with those changes?
5	What makes our organization unique? How can we take advantage of our unique attributes?
6	What special circumstances will affect us in the next five years specific to funding sources, legislation, goods and services, and public opinion?
7	How will we receive our funds during the next five years? What should be our primary funding sources five years hence?
8	What technological advances will affect our ability to provide better services?
9	How much risk do we want to take, and how much are we willing to take, in the next five years?

Table 2.2: Force Field Analysis to Assess Goal Priority Order

GOAL	Forces That Help Achieve the Goal	Forces That Impede Reaching The Goal	Strategies That Strengthen Goal Achievement	Strategies That Weaken Goal Achievement

Once there is a clearer understanding of the dynamics that will either help you achieve or impede yor goals, then the planning group is in a better position to place the goals in some priority order. Again, there are a variety of ways to accomplish this task. One process is to rank the goals that have been identified in some order by number—with "1" being the highest. Then, in a second column, planning committee members would weigh each goal by assigning a percentage of the organization's resources that they think should be budgeted to each of the goals listed. Of course, the total should equal 100 percent.

Table 2.3 illustrates such a method. One then could assign a weighted rank to each goal using the rank order and weight that each planning committee member identified. One simply would average the weight for each goal for the planning group and then order the rank accordingly. Once the goals are placed in priority order, the average percentage weight of resources is an initial indication of the amount of agency resources that ought to be allocated to achieving that goal.

Table 2.3: Rank Ordering Goals by Attributed Resources

GOAL	RANK	WEIGHT (percent)
1.	5	25
2.	3	20
3.	6	10
4.	1	20
5.	2	15
6.	4	10

Objectives

Objectives are short-term (projected about one year into the future) statements of expected results. Objectives are measurable and observable. While a goal is a statement of a long-range (five years or more) future condition, an objective is a concrete statement of results. Setting the organizational goals and writing objectives (at least two for each goal) is the most critical step in the planning process. Without well-articulated objectives, organizations are hard pressed to insure that appropriate action steps (tactics) are articulated. When writing objectives, be sure that the data which was gathered is at hand, and that the organizational capabilities are well identified.

Objectives are based on the goals that have been identified, and are written in observable and measurable terms with expected results. Once the objectives are refined, they are placed in priority order and are presented to the chief executive officer (or whomever is responsible for approval within the responsibility chart) for approval.

As objectives are developed, be certain to consider the following:

- the agency's mission
- the goals that were developed and placed in priority order
- the needs of the offender population
- the weaknesses of the current system, as well as the organization's capabilities and limitations
- community factors and the organization's ability to change its paradigm

As part of the planning process, be certain to involve all who are affected by the objectives that are written. Staff, volunteers, and sometimes even offenders, should be included in the planning process to design the objectives for the organization. It is important to determine what each unit can do to help the organization reach its goals and objectives.

Finally, setting priorities for each objective within each of the system's units is fundamental to the success of the planning product. When setting priorities, it is important to determine which of the objectives must be accomplished, assigning these an "A" priority. Those objectives that would make it easier for the organization to reach its goals, but can be temporarily delayed, are assigned a "B" priority. Objectives we would like to accomplish, that is, those that are desirable but could be eliminated or postponed, are assigned a "C" priority and are heeded only after A and B priorities have been accomplished.

Objectives are not difficult to write as long as you focus on end results rather than the means to an end. It is critically important to insure that objectives are written concisely, in measurable and observable terms expressing end results. The following seven-step process will aid the planning committee in defining objectives:

Step 1: **Determine Result Areas.** These are the factors that will yield successful outcomes for the program. In the case of youthful offenders, it is often related to the criminogenic needs that we already have discussed. As such, result areas may include reduced recidivism, less aggressive behavior, increased academic achievement, job readiness, and prosocial skill interactions.

Step 2: **Determine Measurement Indicators.** Once result areas are determined, they need to be quantified. Quantified result areas are the measurement indicators that are used in writing objectives. The measurement indicators show how well the program is doing, given each objective. For example, results on academic achievement tests would qualify as a measurement indicator for the academic achievement result area. Learning a specific number of cognitive skills would constitute a measurement indicator for the prosocial skill interaction result area.

Step 3: **Determine Performance Standards.** Performance standards further define the degree of success by detailing how much or little of the measurement indicator should be accomplished in order to be successful. As such, criteria or minimal standards are set as indices of success for each objective.

Step 4: **Determine the Time Frames.** This indicator identifies the amount of time that is allotted to reach the defined performance standards. It is the deadline that is established for the objective to be met.

Step 5: **Determine the Cost Frames.** How much will it cost to meet the specifics of the objective? What amount of money does the organization wish to spend on the objective?

Step 6: **Write the Objective.** If the planning participants completed each of the previous steps, then this step is accomplished easily. It simply requires combining all of the data for each step into one cogent sentence. We suggest the following format be used to write each objective:

To (action verb and statement that reflects the **Measurement Indicator**) by **(Performance Standard)** by **(Deadline)** at a cost of no more than **(Cost Frame)**.

An example for our purposes using this format might be as follows:

To reduce recidivism of youthful offenders who score at least Level Three on the LSI-Y by 60 percent using a cognitive-behavior program intervention within six months after their release, at a cost of no more than $1,800.00 per offender.

Step 7: **Evaluate the Objective.** Review the objective to assess whether it reflects the amount of change desired in the result area, as described in the goals of the plan. If it does, consider the objective operational. If it does not, then revisit the measurement indicator and/or the performance standards to insure they accurately reflect desirable outcomes.

How do the planning committee members know their objectives are operational and targeted effectively? Very often, planning processes yield too many objectives, almost creating objectives for mundane activities within the organization. Lakein (1973) stated the 80/20 rule of effective planning; that 80 percent of productive output emanates from 20 percent of the work input. The remaining 20 percent of productive output comes from the remaining 80 percent of the input (*see* Chart 2.4).

Chart 2.4: The 80/20 Rule of Effective Planning

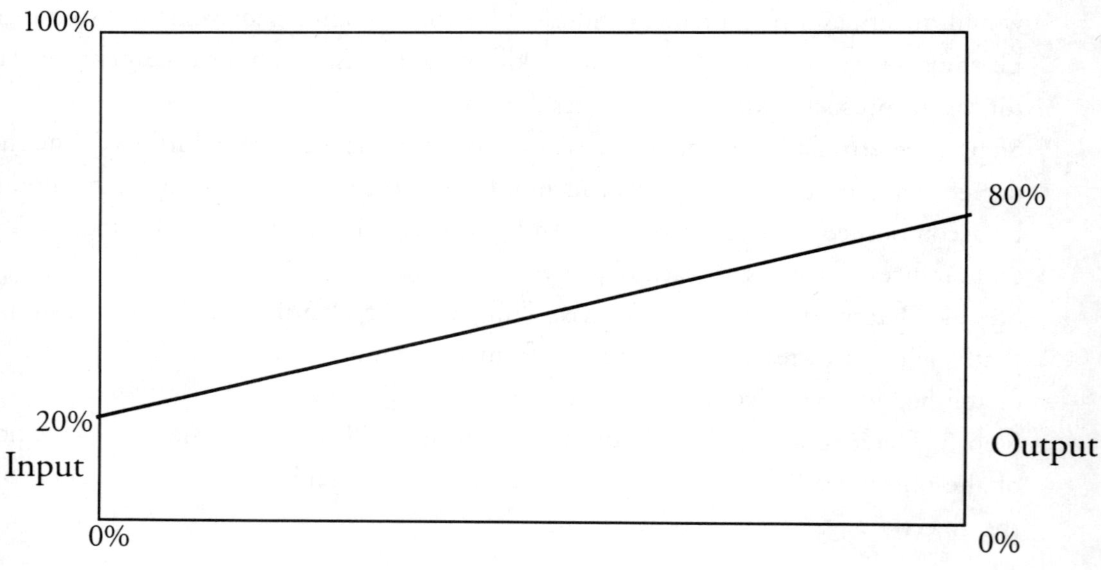

The 80/20 rule has tremendous implication for the planning committee members. Simply, 80 percent of the planning process product will emerge from 20 percent of their effort. Also, do not spend a whole lot of time writing objectives, since according to this rule, 80 percent of the agency's output is not as important as the 20 percent of the product that actually yields 80 percent of the results. Concentrate on the 20 percent to maximize that effort. The manager or group leader should know from the group members and participants who is producing what. The manager knows which members produce assignments of sufficient quality and in a timely manner.

Evaluate and Reassess

Once the planning process has been completed and the implementation plan developed and initiated, it is incumbent on the planning committee to evaluate how the plan is being implemented. Reassessing the plan, as designed, is a useful management tool, and important to the overall planning process. Managers will want to reassess the organization's environment, and individual goals and objectives, comparing the implementation with its actual progress. Thus, it is critically important to be specific and detailed, that is to note who does what, when, and how. The precise and detailed implementation plan will allow managers to target exactly where in the planning process the organization is, and what needs to be redesigned or tweaked, to insure that the plan is implemented successfully.

The manager must review each of the goals and objectives referring the status and assessment of each to the individual who is responsible for its completion. Delegating the responsibility for successful implementation of the specific planning activity back to the one assigned to it insures appropriate accountability and credibility for the entire planning process.

Implementation Plans

Implementation plans are the manifestation of management plans. In essence, they are the detailed tactics of what will happen, when, who will implement it, and how. Since we detail an illustration of a specific implementation plan in the next section, we merely will reference here the importance for all staff to participate in the design and development of an implementation plan. This document is the management tool that all staff will reference on the programs and services that are delivered to the youthful offender. There are several useful tools that aid in charting implementation plans. These include Pert Charts, Gantt Charts, time lines, and a table of objectives, each then listing who does what, when, and how.

Pert and Gantt Charts

Pert and Gantt charts are flow charts that show the process and progress of the management plan. An example of this type of implementation plan is Chart 2.2, in which we depicted the management planning process. Usually, there are several conventions that are used in this type of charting. These include the following:

These are a few examples of the more popular and common symbols used in charting.

Denotes Process, for example: read policy and procedure; calculate risk scores

Denotes Decision Point

Denotes Data

Denotes Document

Denotes Multiple Documents

Time Lines

This implementation planning technique is most useful when outlining or displaying a summary of events. Again, the pertinent information of who does what, how, and when is built into the time line. Most project applications include this utility tool within its drop-down menu files. Most time lines follow the convention in highlighting those events in regular intervals such as weeks or months. In longer management plans spanning five years or more, the data also may be displayed on an annual time line.

Table of Objectives

Each objective in the management plan is placed on a separate sheet of paper within the implementation plan. Under each objective, a table is created that includes the pertinent information of who does what, when, and how. Table 2.4 illustrates how this is accomplished.

Table 2.4: Objective - To insure that each new admission receives a medical examination within seven days of arrival at the institution.

WHAT	*WHO*	*WHEN*	*HOW*
Identify new admissions	Intake secretary	Upon arrival	Generate intake list within computer data base
Schedule medical appointment	Unit manager *(for example, sergeant)*	Within 24 hours of arrival	Call infirmary charge nurse for appointment
Conduct admission medical examination	Physician or physician's assistant	At scheduled appointment	Medical practice
Report results	Physician or charge nurse	Within 24 hours after examination	Input into computer data base

Conclusion

This section described the planning process and its importance to the operations of the organization. We have attempted to demonstrate that a sound strategic plan, developed by a well-coordinated planning process, bolsters staff commitment to the organization. It also improves staff interaction; articulates the organization's mission, goals, and objectives so that each is understood by the entire system; and provides opportunities for administrators and managers to supervise the agency's operations more efficiently and effectively. It is the planning process and the strategic plan that is developed that ultimately provides the foundation on which programs are developed and implemented for the violent youthful offender placed in adult correctional systems. Without a reliable, prudent, and sanctioned plan, organizations are handicapped in their ability to provide effective and efficient youth programs.

Chapter 3

Managing the Process

"F@# YOU! You can't make me do sh*t. Oh yeah, try it, and I will mess you over real bad."*

— Youth responding to a correctional officer's directive

"Your mother is like a police station. Dicks running in and out."

"Your mother is like a door knob, everyone gets a turn"

"Your mother is so low, she has to look up at the belly of a pregnant ant."

— Two youths playing the dozens

Introduction

Thus far, we have provided the foundation and rationale under which youthful offenders are placed in adult corrections systems. We have reviewed the parameters on which youthful offenders have been adjudicated and incarcerated, and we have explained the various statutes, regulations, policies, and procedures that affect youthful offender placement. We also have devoted a major portion of this monograph to the planning process and the function it plays in helping implement effective youthful offender programs. In this section, we will highlight and detail a variety of techniques, strategies, and tactics that can make the implementation of youthful offender programs and services easier.

We also will enumerate specific ideas to assist administrators in managing the system to serve youthful offenders. The objective is to provide line staff with techniques to better manage youthful offender behavior and deliver appropriate programs and services. It is important for managers and their staff to understand that there are certain approaches, tasks, and skills, that, when acquired and used, will enhance the quality of services provided to the youthful offenders. In addition, these approaches will help enhance the line staff's ability to accomplish their tasks with fewer critical incidents, less difficulty, and greater efficiency and effectiveness. After reading this, managers will be better prepared to supervise programs and personnel to insure effective operations throughout their entire system. Line staff will be better prepared to implement programs and services with confidence and integrity.

This section is a guide and a resource for correctional staff and those students of correctional systems to use as they pursue the challenge of providing programs and services to youthful offenders. We begin by providing frameworks for action. Understanding these strategic approaches increases staff ability to implement management plans and agency policy. As such, specific examples that illustrate key factors of these systems will be provided. The reader is encouraged to modify these examples, as their systems require. However, understanding the fundamental principles will establish the benchmarks on which sound, effective, and efficient youthful offender programs can be implemented.

Framework for Action: The Program Implementation Window

How do staff within a correctional system—whether it is a preincarceration/probation function, an institution, a community-based program, or an aftercare/parole function—organize programs for effective implementation? One useful technique is shown in Chart 3.1, the Program Implementation Window. This framework organizes all functions, strategies, and tactics into four frames: paper, people, places, and materials. With this conceptual model, all tasks, program interventions, and ensuing action may be categorized according to these frames.

Chart 3.1 The Program Implementation Window

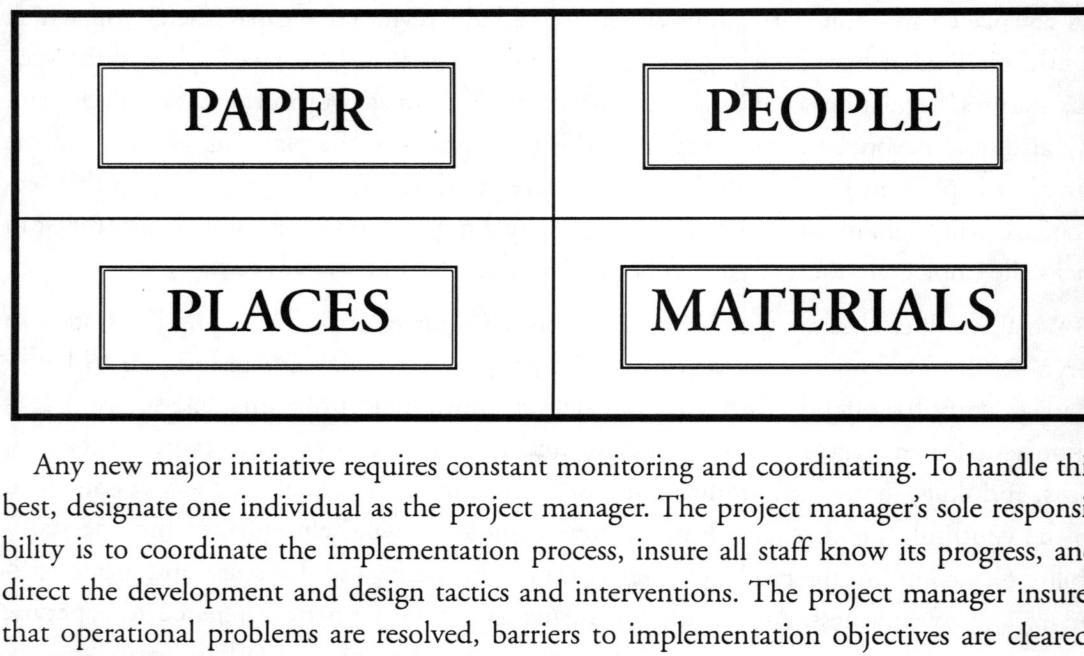

Any new major initiative requires constant monitoring and coordinating. To handle this best, designate one individual as the project manager. The project manager's sole responsibility is to coordinate the implementation process, insure all staff know its progress, and direct the development and design tactics and interventions. The project manager insures that operational problems are resolved, barriers to implementation objectives are cleared, and flexibility of the program design is maintained.

The implementation plan, which should be well distributed throughout the system, is the primary document that all staff consults as the program is incrementally implemented. A well-detailed implementation plan is based on the mission, goals, and objectives that were developed for the youthful offender program and includes:

- a list of actions, events, or tasks that needs to be completed
- a list of persons who will be responsible for specifics of each action, event, or task listed
- the date by which the action, the event, or the task is to be completed
- information on how the action, the event, or the task will be completed

The plan is a dynamic document that should be consulted consistently and frequently as the youthful offender program is implemented. It is a tool that the project manager, along with all staff, will use to insure the intricate parts of the institution are well coordinated, since every part of the institution is impacted when a new program or service is introduced.

We now explain and provide examples of how the various parts of an implementation plan may be configured within the planning window (Chart 3.2). This gives the project manager a paradigm with which to approach his or her task.

Once the tasks and issues are listed in the appropriate quadrants of the planning window, each may be further detailed and elaborated on to form the implementation plan that will be used by all staff. We have provided some examples of the detail for each of the quadrants. As you review the illustrations provided, note that for each task or issue listed, there is a specific set of actions that identify who does what, when, and how. These tactical interventions support the strategic plan that is developed.

PAPER

SPECIFIC ACTIONS/EVENTS/TASKS

Detail the exact number of new or revised policies and procedures that will be needed prior to the implementation of the program. List the name of the policy and the procedure.

State the rationale for the revision or creation of the policy or procedure. State the rationale for requiring this policy and procedure prior to the implementation of the program. Then, develop a detailed schedule for the completion of needed policies and procedures. The schedule should take into account any setbacks that may occur in drafting, writing, getting approval, and printing. Be sure to build enough time into the schedule to account for unforeseen delays or unplanned events. There may be other steps in the policy and procedure process in your agency, so be sure to add these processes into your schedule. *See Developing Policies and Procedures for Jails* (1996) for useful information on how to formulate these items.

PERSON(S) RESPONSIBLE FOR ACTIONS/EVENTS/TASKS

When identifying the person(s) responsible for accomplishing the actions/events/tasks, identify the person(s) to whom the actions/events/tasks have been assigned and also the person(s) actually tasked with completing them. For example, the deputy director for administration is given the responsibility to write and print the new or revised policies and procedures for the youthful offender program. However, in reality, the deputy director will delegate those subtasks to specific individuals who will perform the actual functions. It is important for the person who is responsible for coordinating the implementation of the program and for the persons who actually are tasked with the functions to know each other so that if there are any problems or issues, they can communicate directly with each other. This must be a team effort!

Chart 3.2 —Youthful Offender Program Planning Window

1. PAPER	2. PEOPLE
Policies, Procedures, Post Orders Departmental - Review/Adapt/Create Institutional - Review/Adapt/Create <u>Areas of Concern</u> Special Management Unit Sanctions Assignment to Specific Programs: Canteen, Mail, Phone Calls Removal from Program, and so forth. Program Operational/Administrative Manuals Case Management Forms, Other Forms, Orientation Packets, Evaluation Forms, Dietary Menus	Staff (Institutional) Staff (Agency Support) Youthful Offenders Youthful Offenders' Families Courts and Legal Community Governmental Agencies Other Correctional Agencies Volunteers
3. PLACES	**4. MATERIALS**
Reception and Evaluation Living Areas Program Areas Educational Areas Recreational Areas Central/Regional Offices Out of Facility courts medical	Security Perimeter/Exterior, Interior Officer Clothing -Uniforms - (Image) Programs Youthful Offender Orientation Videotape Agriculture/Work Programs Youthful Offender Clothing (to include footwear) Transportation Food Service Recreational Supplies Physical Plant

CHRONOLOGICAL ORDER OF ACTIONS/EVENTS/TASKS

Identifying the chronological order of actions/events/tasks is important because it requires the people who are responsible for the design and implementation of the program to think about and justify the order in which actions, events, and tasks need to take place. Very often, when this process is followed, those responsible discover that what has been proposed is not possible in the time frames that have been assigned to that process.

This may be because the agency does not have the resources, or those agency resources have been committed to a different mission for that time period. The implementation guide may have staff assigned to a specific task only to find out that the same staff is assigned to a different place. Another issue that the implementation plan can uncover is that a specific staff person may be assigned to different actions, events, and tasks at the same time. For example, the schedule states that all policies and procedures will be submitted to the director for approval during the first week of May. However, the director's schedule indicates that she will be out of town that week attending mandatory training.

Another advantage to identifying the chronological order of actions, events, and tasks that are to be accomplished is that this precludes "logjams." Logjams occur when one action, event, or task that was scheduled does not take place, thereby causing other actions, events, and tasks to be stalled and conflict with each other. This type of misstep causes confusion and frustration among the staff and youthful offenders. Another negative aspect of logjams is that they sap the momentum from the process. Too many logjams may compromise the goals and objectives of the program, placing them in jeopardy of ever being accomplished. (Example: Youthful offenders are being detained in the reception center because the director has not approved the policy and procedure on youthful offender classification. Therefore, no youthful offenders can leave the reception center, which causes crowding and security problems there, and idle staff who are assigned to the youthful offender facility.)

PEOPLE

SPECIFIC ACTIONS, EVENTS, AND TASKS

Identify the number and type of staff who will be needed to implement the program. The implementation plan also must take into account the following:

- any training requirements necessary for the staff
- promotional boards (length of time advertisements must be posted)
- appointments related to staffing requirements of the program
- staff transfers and relocation (time and expenses)

- adjustments due to staff vacations
- internal and external recruitment (length of time for these processes)

Staff selection and training is one of the most important areas to consider when implementing a youthful offender program. The program's goals and objectives will dictate the number and types of staff who will be needed to accomplish those goals and objectives. The exact number and rank of security staff, program staff, administrative staff, educational staff, and support staff need to be identified and justified.

A word of caution: do not depend on traditional staffing models for adult facilities. They are not applicable. Rather, base the youthful offender program staffing on this question: What type of staff is needed to accomplish the stated goals and objectives of the youthful offender program in the most cost-effective and efficient manner possible?

Person(s) Responsible for Actions, Events, and Tasks

Without question, the assignment of people to specific tasks is the most difficult part of developing the implementation plan. The entire success of the program may be jeopardized if one person does not accomplish the tasks he or she has been assigned within the allotted time period.

As mentioned previously, if the deputy director is assigned the responsibility to accomplish a specific task, she or he usually assigns the actual performance of the task to a subordinate. In some cases, the subordinate who has been assigned the task does not understand what must be done and/or does not realize that there is a time frame in which the task should be accomplished. All staff should be encouraged to communicate directly with the implementation program plan coordinator. In turn, the program plan coordinator should frequently contact staff assigned specific tasks. By doing this, the person responsible for the task will have a clear understanding of what he or she is supposed to do and when it must be done.

Always have a back-up staff person to complete task assignments. Correctional systems are dynamic and ever-changing. It is inevitable that people get moved, promoted, or are unable to complete their task assignment. Thus, when assigning people to tasks, ensure that each person assigned has a back-up staff person to complete the task should the original person be unable or unwilling to do so.

Chronological Order of the Action, Events, and Tasks

The chronological order of the people quadrant can tend to be a bit complicated in that there are people who will be used to plan the program, implement, and operate it. So, as the process progresses chronologically, some people are added and some people leave. The critical tactic is twofold: do not bring people on too early; and do not let people go too soon. Because the staff is the single most expensive commodity within any program budget, it is important to use the right people at the right time. We suggest that during the implementation planning phase, the team should be comprised of those at the level of the director or commissioner, such as wardens, deputy wardens, majors, captains, supervisory counselors, school principals, classification supervisors, and head nurses. As the process progresses through the planning and implementation phase, these teams may be changed, expanded, or reduced to meet the needs of the planning and implementation functions.

Planning teams can be costly to the organization because they require staff to participate in activities other than their assigned roles. However, delegating planning responsibilities to responsible staff creates involvement and staff empowerment. The benefits of having staff involved at all levels of the process far outweighs the liabilities. Staff, once empowered, also will self-select the degree to which they need to be involved with the process. Even when staff cease to be involved with the formal planning structure, their own contributions to the process increase their need to be advised of the program's progress. In the long run, this is a great administrative tool. Investing staff in program development insures continued quality of service to youth in care. Additionally, this tactic increases team efforts and productivity.

Places

Specific Actions, Events, and Tasks

The implementation team must identify where the program will be housed. To make this determination, the team must look at the goals and objectives of the program. If, for example, the program will have a work component as part of it, then the facility where it is going to be housed must have sufficient work activities for all the youthful offenders in the program.

The team also must review the facility where the program is going to be housed and identify any repairs, additions, or modifications that will need to occur before the youthful offenders move into the facility. If the facility already houses youthful offenders, then the team still needs to insure that the physical plant meets the goals and objectives of the program. If the team finds that there are discrepancies between the goals and objectives of the program and the facility's ability to provide the necessary space, staff, and support, then the team should make recommendations to correct these discrepancies so that the goal and objectives of the program will be met. If the discrepancies cannot be corrected, the team should look for another facility to house the program.

South Carolina designed its Youthful Offender Program with three phases. Phase one and two were housed at the Wateree Correctional Institution, which also is one of the oldest facilities in the system. The implementation team felt that the facility had all the physical requirements necessary to meet the goals and objectives of the program. Specifically, it had a farm that the youthful offenders could work, and it had sufficient space in the educational area for the youthful offenders to attend school. Both work and school were cornerstones of the program. We wish to emphasize that the age of the facility is not critical. Rather, the physical plant first must be able to accommodate the mission, goals, and objectives of the program, as developed and designed.

Person(s) Responsible for Actions, Events, and Tasks

As the implementation team identifies areas in the physical plant that may preclude the program from achieving its goals, it also has to also identify the people who will correct the situation. The nature of the deficiencies will dictate who should be assigned the tasks to correct them. For instance, if the corrections are minor, it is possible that the warden can use the institutional budget to correct the identified deficiencies. On the other hand, if the corrections are significant and it will take the approval of the commissioner, then possibly the deputy commissioner in charge of that area can correct the situation. The tasks for getting the necessary corrections made to the physical plant must be assigned to the appropriate staff person(s) and a time frame to accomplish the corrections must be established.

As tasks are assigned to staff, be sure that one person does not get too many tasks assigned to her or him. This is something that can happen very easily, especially if the organization is small. In this case, one individual is perceived as competent to get the tasks completed quickly and effectively.

Chronological Order of the Events, Actions, and Tasks

One realizes the importance of planning events/actions/tasks chronologically when dealing with correcting physical plant deficiencies. This is because in many cases, the team and the organization have to depend on outside resources. An example of this may be if the organization has to go out to bid for some materials to correct a deficiency. The implementation team then must start to make some important decisions. Should they delay the implementation stage of the program while they wait for the necessary materials to correct the physical plant, or can they proceed with the implementation plan and make the corrections to the physical plant later? If a team has to face a situation like this and they decide to move forward with other parts of the implementation plan, they have to make sure that they recalculate the completion date/events/action/tasks that have been delayed. The team should not lose its attention to the detail, as originally stated in the implementation plan.

Materials and Technology

Specific Actions, Events, and Tasks

The materials and technology quadrant of the planning window presents special challenges for the planning coordinator and design team. Materials alone encompass such items as youthful offender clothing, cleaning supplies, educational books and aids, and religious articles to name but a few. Technology may include video surveillance cameras in the living area, computers for the classroom, transportation security devices, and vocational equipment. Again, the team must use the stated goals and objectives of the program as a guide and for direction. The implementation plan must include specific detail as to when materials should be ordered, delivered, installed, or where they will be stored for future use. This should include all support materials such as program-related forms used by the staff in the program.

The implementation team must be precise when identifying the materials needed to accomplish the goals and objectives of the program. For example, one youthful offender program issued the youthful offenders the same canvas type shoe that was issued to all the other youthful offenders. The youthful offenders in the program were required to march, do close-order drill, and perform physical training. After a short period of time, the staff associated with the program realized that there was an increase in youthful offenders going on sick-call with lower extremity and foot problems and that the shoes were wearing out prematurely. During the planning process, the shoes that the youthful offenders were to wear were never evaluated. As such, the quality of the product was never assessed. Hence, there were problems with youthful offenders who became injured, and the poor product reliability presented serious operational issues.

The use of security equipment such as video cameras, fence detection systems, and staff two-way radios can affect the efficiency of the staff. Youthful offenders present unique and new challenges for adult correctional institutions, so any method that can be employed to assist the staff should be given serious consideration by the implementation team. Youthful offenders demand more personal attention from the staff. This personal attention can cause breaches in typical routine and security practices so any technology that can be installed to assist the staff will benefit the program.

Now that we have reviewed the components of paper, people, places, materials, and technology, and the elements of an implementation plan, we will combine all of these elements in the following illustration (Chart 3.3 pages 62-64). The following example involves moving youthful offenders to the facility for the first day of operation of the program.

Chart 3.3: Elements Involved in Moving Youthful Offenders

Time	Actions/Tasks/Events	Persons Responsible
05:00	Staff role call	Associate Wardens (AW) for security and programs
05:15	Call transportation for final numbers	AW/Security
05:20	Youthful offenders: receiving informed of numbers	AW/Security
05:20	Youthful offenders: receiving prepares basic issues	Supply sgt.
05:20	Final walk through inspection	Lt., Sgts., COs
05:30	Security staff assume posts	Sgts. and COs
05:30	Perimeter fence and sensor checked	Sgt. and COs
05:30	Kitchen informed of numbers of youthful offenders arriving	AW/Security
05:30	Breakfast meal being prepared	Food service supervisor
05:45	Youthful offenders arrive	Warden, AWs,
		All youthful offender program staff
06:00	Youthful offenders in-process	Warden, AWs, Capt., Lt., Sgts., COs, Programs
	Youthful offender rule book and program rules distributed	Lt., Sgts., COs
	Youthful offenders are assigned to living area	Classification
06:45	Youthful offenders moved to living areas	Sgts. and COs
06:50	Youthful offenders drop off uniforms, etc. in living area	Sgts. and COs
07:00	Youthful offenders move to breakfast	Lt., Sgts. and COs
07:10	Youthful offenders eat breakfast	(AW)s, Cpt., Lt., Sgts., and COs
07:20	Youthful offenders move from dining room to intake testing	Lt., Sgts. and COs
07:30	Youthful offender testing begins	Medical staff, Sgt., and COs

Chart 3.3: Elements Involved in Moving Youthful Offenders (continued)

Time	Actions/Tasks/Events	Persons responsible
09:00	Youthful offenders are moved from medical to living area	Sgt. and COs
09:10	Youthful offenders in living area dayroom	Sgt. and COs
09:15	Explanation given of the rules, regulations, and expectations of the program	Warden/AW
	Personal conduct	Captain
	Maintenance of personal living area	Lt.
	Purpose and phases of the program	Captain
	Chain of command	Sgt.
	Day-to-day operations and expectations	COs
	Education overview	School principal
	Overview of programs	AW for programs
	Medical overview and sick call procedures	Nurse
11:30	Youthful offenders move to noon meal	Lt., Sgts., and COs
11:40	Youthful offenders' noon meal	Captain, Lt., Sgt., and COs
12:00	Youthful offenders move to living area	Lt., Sgts., COs
12:10	Youthful offenders prepare living area	Sgts. and COs
	Youthful offenders make-up beds	Sgts. and COs
	Youthful offenders set up personal locker	Sgts. and COs
14:15	Practice inspection of youthful offender living area	Lt., Sgts., COs
15:00	Youthful offenders move to physical training	Sgt. and COs
15:15	Youthful offenders have physical education (rec. yard)	Sgt. and COs

Chart 3.3: Elements Involved in Moving Youthful Offenders (continued)

Time	Actions/Tasks/Events	Persons responsible
15:50	Youthful offenders move to living area	Sgts. and COs
16:00	Youthful offenders shower and have free time	Sgts. and COs
16:50	Youthful offenders move to evening meal	Lt., Sgts., and COs
17:00	Youthful offenders' evening meal	Captain, Lt., Sgts., and COs
17:30	Youthful offenders move from evening meal	Lt., Sgts., and COs
17:40	Youthful offenders meet with personal counselor in living area	Sgts. and COs
20:00	Youthful offenders prepare for lights out	Sgts. and COs
20:30	Standing formal count	Lt., Sgts., and COs
20:45	Lock-down, lights out	Captain, Lt., Sgts., and COs

The implementation plan is a staff tool. Administrators would use the implementation plan to help manage the process as the program is developed, keeping staff focused on their tasks and insuring accountability for task completion. Supervisors would use the plan to direct day-to-day operations and insure that each staff person accomplished his or her particular assignment in an effective and efficient manner. Staff would use the plan to remind them of their daily obligations while structuring their time to insure the program is maintained for the population. All staff will use the document as a catalyst for change, a positive reinforcement for the accomplishments, and a tool to keep them on target. We now turn to each activity to illustrate how the plan may be detailed.

Staff Role Call

The staff roll call is a meeting convened by the deputy wardens for security and programs. It involves all the staff who are assigned to the youthful offender program or have involvement in any way with it. During these daily staff roll call meetings, specific operational issues for the day are reviewed so that all staff members know when, where, and what they are to do throughout the day. Other important items such as policies, procedures, population count, untoward incidents that may have happened, special events, or other information is shared. Since we know from the adolescent development model that youthful offenders perceive their world in a holistic manner, it is critical that all staff understand both the program and security issues of the day. Hence, there is the need to have both program and security deputies involved in the meeting, with each having equal authority and commitment.

Youthful Offender Receiving Area

The youthful offender receiving area is the first exposure the youth has to the institution. As such, it should appear well organized, friendly, yet business like. By the time the youths arrive, as noted in the schedule, the youthful offender receiving area already will have been informed of the number of youthful offenders in transit and will have prepared the basic orientation packages for each. These include:

- two blankets
- two sheets
- one pillow
- one pillow case
- one pair of boots
- three towels
- three face cloths
- one can of shoe polish
- three rags (for polishing shoes)
- three uniforms (the agency will decide on the type of uniform that will be worn by the youthful offenders)
- outerwear (jacket, gloves, hats, sweaters, and so forth)
- toiletries (the type of toiletries that will be permitted will be decided by the implementation team prior to the start of the program)

Final Walk-through Inspection

The implementation team conducts a final walk-through inspection of the program areas that include education, recreation, counseling, dining, and living sections. The purpose of the review is to insure that every detail necessary to operate the program is in place, and if there are missing elements, that an individual is assigned to correct the situation in a timely manner. Any object that is not needed for the youthful offenders' direct use in the program should be removed. These may include:

- mops
- mop buckets
- brooms

- books and magazines
- cleaning supplies
- extra mattresses
- things left behind by maintenance crews

Security Staff Assume Posts

The security staff assume their posts as the implementation team completes its inspection of the program areas. On assuming their posts, each security officer assigned to any post should read the post orders for that post. They also should check the daily schedule to insure that they know when and where they are supposed to be during the day. For the youthful offender program, in particular, we strongly recommend that the security staff should not have fixed posts. Instead, security officers should be assigned a group of youthful offenders and the officers should move with their assigned groups.

Perimeter Fence and Sensor Check

Similar to the program walk through, the perimeter fence and sensor check is a final inspection of the security for the youthful offenders and their program. Again, deficiencies should be noted and corrected, assigning the task to a specific individual of the implementation team. The following areas of the perimeter fence should be observed:

- condition of the fencing material
  Is it well maintained?
  Is the fence material connected to the poles at appropriate intervals?
  Is it secured to the baseline (either by cement or by a pole that runs along the base line of the fencing material)?
- conditions of fence poles and whether they are spaced appropriately and are securely anchored (all nuts and bolts are in place and secure)
- condition of the razor ribbon
  Is it attached to the fence properly, securely, and at the correct intervals?
  Is it installed at a correct height?
  Double check to insure that none of the material is hanging loosely or dangling.

Kitchen Staff Informed of Final Number of Youth

Information sharing with relevant program areas continues by informing the kitchen staff of the number of youthful offenders expected in the program. Appropriate information allows the food services staff to prepare adequate types and quantities of food for the youthful offender population. Also, security staff need to monitor this operation especially well since this is a potential area where youth and adult offenders interact.

Youthful Offenders Arrive

There are two scenarios under which youthful offenders arrive at their program. The first is when the program is brand new and is receiving youth for the first time. The second is when the program already has a youthful offender population, and new youthful offenders are arriving for the first time. Security staff should greet the new arrivals with dignity, respect, and deliberate direction. The correctional officers, along with program staff, should communicate confidence of purpose, without intimidation and harassment. There need be no yelling at the youthful offenders or diminution of the offenders.

Rather, just as the program has been designed with deliberate structure and decisive thought, so the new arrivals should be greeted with specific instructions of welcome. They should be informed about where they are to assemble, what the next several hours will entail, and how each of the youthful offenders is to behave in relation to each other and to staff (in other words, no hitting, no talking without permission, address staff by last names or rank and name, or "yes sir," "yes ma'am"). The watchword is that this is the youthful offender's first impression of how they should interact and behave while they are participants in the youthful offender program.

Youthful Offenders In-process

The youthful offenders should participate in an orientation program as soon as possible after they arrive at the institution. In our schedule, it is the first day, within an hour after they arrive. The orientation process has several parts. The warden begins the session and provides the youthful offenders with the mission of the program and the expectations the staff have of them while they are in the institution. The warden's message is one of hope for the future, in that each of the youthful offenders has the ability to take this experience as a learning experience, no matter how long their incarceration. The assistant wardens for program and security then address the group. They follow the vision outlined by the warden providing specifics for each of their areas. As such, the security assistant warden speaks of a safe environment, one that does not tolerate verbal aggression or physical hostilities. The program assistant warden speaks of the variety of programs that include education, counseling, religious activities, leisure time activities, and recreation. We now detail other important components of the orientation to the institution.

Breakfast

Movement of youth to all parts of the program is critically important. As such, there should be sufficient staff available to supervise the youth as they move through the institution without incident among themselves, or with others. Once the youthful offenders are at the dining area, they should be reinstructed on how to move through the serving line.

Have a staff person go first, to model for those who follow. Also, youthful offenders are skill-deficient (*see* the adolescent development model) and require structure and direction in these areas. Consider the following suggested rules for the dining area:

- No talking during meals (talking can be a privilege that can be earned as youthful offenders successfully move through the program).
- Youthful offenders must sit with their group.
- Youthful offenders are not permitted to get up from their seats until everyone in their group is finished, and then only with the permission of a sergeant or correctional officer.
- When the youthful offenders leave the dining room, they should go outside and line up in their group. Prepare a place or procedure for this inside, in case of inclement weather.

Medical/Dental Testing

Youthful offenders entering the youthful offender program must have complete and thorough physical and dental examinations. Medical testing ensures that the youthful offender is free from contagious disease and can withstand the rigors of certain aspects of the program. It is advantageous for the medical staff to keep the program staff informed of what the youthful offender is able to do in the program rather than just citing what they are prohibited from doing. Again, the medical staff should use the adolescent development concepts to make these assessments.

Living Area

We suggest that youthful offenders begin this phase of their orientation in the living area dayroom, or the general meeting room for the living unit. The security captains for the housing unit should greet the youths in a group and review what the offenders may expect for the rest of the day. Other living area staff will be introduced to the youthful offenders and the chain of command will be reviewed. Youths are encouraged to use the staff to help solve problems, and they should learn that the person at the top does not necessarily have the answers to their questions, nor the power to immediately resolve their problems.

The youthful offenders are instructed by the sergeants and correctional officers, with whom they will have intensive day-to-day contact, about how to behave appropriately and how to clean and maintain the living areas and dayroom that they will be occupying. The youths also will receive instructions on how to use certain systems that have been set up for them to resolve problems or issues. Examples of these forms are as follows:

- The form that the youthful offenders will use to request to see the warden or deputy warden—explain where those forms are kept and where they are to be deposited.
- Youthful offender grievance system—explain where these forms are kept and where they are to be deposited.
- Forms for replacement of clothing or bedding—explain where these forms are kept and where they are to be deposited.

Rule Book, Program Rules, and Youthful Offender Program Rules

A written set of rules outlining the behavioral expectations of the youthful offenders should be published and provided to each offender. For all components of the program (security, education, vocational education, counseling, medical, ministerial, food services, recreation, and housing) staff should present their section of the rule book to the offender group. Some of the specifics of a rule book should include the following:

- Personal conduct. Topics included in this section may include:
  - how to address staff and other youthful offenders
  - how to question a directive
  - how to properly wear clothing
  - how to deal with confrontational situations
  - how to deal with anger
  - personal hygiene
  - behavior in the dining area
  - behavior in the living area
- Maintenance of personal areas. The youthful offenders should be shown what an acceptable living area looks like. There should be a checklist for the youthful offenders to ensure that the living areas are cleaned and maintained properly. Sergeants and correctional officers will demonstrate and then assist the youthful offenders with directions on how to make their beds and arrange their lockers in the prescribed manner.
- Purpose of the youthful offender program. This should be explained by either the warden or the director of the youthful facility program.
- Chain of command. Sergeants explain the program's chain of command to the youthful offenders. The youthful offenders must understand that they always must go to the correctional officer who is assigned to their living area with any questions, issues, or problems before they approach any other staff higher in the chain of command.

- Day-to-day operational expectations. Correctional officers should present this section of the rule book because they are in first-line authority with the youthful offenders, and are in the best position to translate the program's goals and objectives into the youths' behaviors and performances.
- Education overview. The principal presents this section and outlines what the educational goals of the program are, with an emphasis on what is required. Because most youthful offenders have not been successful in school, this section can be very uncomfortable for many of them. Many youthful offenders feel that they will not be able to complete the educational program requirements because of their past educational performances and experiences. It is up to the principal to ensure that this presentation is positive and reassuring for the youth. The principal should emphasize that they will be given whatever help, assistance, and guidance they need to complete the educational program. In a firm but positive and reassuring manner, the youthful offenders also must be told that they will have to take responsibility for their own learning.
- Medical and sick call. Nurses and physicians should review these procedures for the youthful offenders, including explaining how to get routine medical care, emergency services, and ongoing medications.

Since it is critically important that all youths understand the rules of the institution, it may be wise to plan several meetings during the first week of the program to review this material. Also, it may be prudent to meet with the youths in smaller groups (perhaps the size of a classroom).

Noon Meal

The sergeants and correctional officers assigned to the program move the youthful offenders in formation to the noon meal. Youthful offenders should be reminded of the behavior that will be required of them while they are in the dining area and during mealtimes. Under no circumstances should the youths be subjected to any kind of ridicule during mealtimes.

Preparing the Living Area

The schedule for this first day is filled with directed activities to provide the youthful offenders with a clear message that there is order to the program and a prescribed action plan. There is time to accomplish all tasks given a plan of action that is well designed and implemented. As such, youthful offenders are given time at this juncture in their day to make their beds and prepare their lockers under the direction of the security staff.

During this time, lieutenants also conduct a practice inspection with both the youths and the correctional staff present. The goal of this activity is to reinforce the positive effort and behaviors of the youths, and to praise the correctional staff for their guidance and direction.

Physical Training

Physical training, education, and recreation are critical to the youthful offender program. Physical training provides important physical activity necessary for the adolescent developmental needs. It also provides a release of energy and stress that the youths build up throughout the day. All activities should be planned, structured, and directed by a well-trained physical education teacher or certified recreation specialist, both of whom have been trained in adolescent development issues. We caution that security personnel should not be the primary staff to organize and implement youth recreation programs.

Showers

Youth are returned to their living area after recreation to clean up and prepare for dinner. The sergeants and correctional officers assigned to the youthful offender living areas must be vigilant during this time, since this is the first time that the youthful offenders will shower in their living area. Security staff should observe the behavior of the offenders and look for youths who are not going to shower, those who may make inappropriate comments, or youthful offenders who become aggressive.

The security staff should approach those youthful offenders who do not seem to want to shower and find out why. In most cases, it is because they are afraid that they might be sexually assaulted or they are just embarrassed (an adolescent development issue) to be naked in front of other people. The security staff should encourage the youthful offenders to shower and assure them that they will be safe in the shower, if that is their fear. It also is helpful to have counselors available during this time to assist the security staff in ensuring that all the youthful offenders shower.

Free Time

The free time that is included in the schedule is exactly that. The youthful offenders should be permitted twenty to thirty minutes of free time. During this period, they should be encouraged to write letters, polish their shoes, talk among themselves, read, and straighten up their living areas. During this free time period, the youthful offenders should not be permitted to sleep or lay on their beds. The youthful offenders should be given a specific time when they should be ready to move to the evening meal. It should be their responsibility to be ready, and if they are not ready then, they should be held accountable according to program sanctions (for example, given extra work details after lights out).

Evening Meal

The evening meal is very important because it is the last meal the youthful offenders will have before breakfast. Therefore, it is crucial that the portions be sufficient and that the caloric count conforms to the requirements of active adolescents. Youthful offenders should be given ample time to eat their meals without harassment. If evening snacks are going to be given to the youthful offenders (which is our recommendation), they could be issued to the youthful offenders at the evening meal. A rule could be in place that says the youthful offenders are not permitted to eat their snacks until a certain time. The shift commander should be present in the dining area while the youthful offenders are eating. If the meals are served in the youthful offenders' living areas, the shift commander should visit every living area during the meal period and ensure that everything is running according to schedule.

Youthful Offenders Meet with their Personal Counselor

During this period of time, each youthful offender meets with his or her personal counselor. Those youthful offenders who do not meet with a counselor should be constructively involved with some aspect of the program or community living tasks. During this first meeting, the counselors inform the youthful offenders about how to contact them with problems, issues, or questions. The counselors should emphasize that they are part of a team of corrections professionals who will be working together on their behalf. The goal of this meeting is to demonstrate to the youthful offenders that all the correctional staff associated with the program are part of a team.

The counselor takes the opportunity at this time to emphasize the team concept and explains how all the staff communicate with each other constantly about the youths and their particular needs. This message is important to reduce manipulation among the youths.

Youthful Offenders Prepare for Lights Out/Lockdown

Staff ensure that all cleaning supplies and equipment are stored by having them return to the area near their bed or cell. Staff should give youthful offenders time to get ready for lights out and/or lockdown. The security staff conducts last minute inspections of the living area and common areas. Since this is the youthful offenders' first night, the security staff should take this opportunity to go over the rules and regulations for after lights out and/or lockdown. Topics that should be covered include how to contact security staff, medical emergencies, and so forth. The security staff should cover anything unique to their facilities.

The staff conducts the last count of the day, which is a standing formal count. The sergeant should verify the count and once the count is cleared, the youthful offenders should be instructed to get into their bunks and their cells should be locked down.

We have attempted to provide a rather detailed explanation and example of an implementation plan for the first day of a youthful offender's arrival at an institution. Even though it seems tedious and perhaps redundant, it is imperative that every movement, activity, and event have a purpose and be planned in advance. Only then will both the staff and the offender realize that this program intends to make a difference in their lives where, previously, little attention and caring were provided.

Framework for Action: Staff—The Backbone of Effective Programs

It is people who make programs effective. In all our administrative experience, one axiom that has been a constant in our work with aggressive and violent youth is that the primary role of a supervisor is to create an environment in which staff can grow, professionally and personally. This is our mantra as we manage any organization. We include this statement of our philosophy in our program descriptions, and we take every opportunity to communicate it openly to staff. The second framework for action underscores the important role staff play in affecting the growth of youthful offenders as they develop through their adolescence. As such, how staff interact with each other, and in turn, with the offender population, is critical to effective programming and the target of our deliberate intervention.

This section begins with a brief history of administrative models. We then describe an effective tool, situational leadership (Hersey and Blanchard, 1977), which has wide application to program implementation issues, including the Youth Development System (described later in this section). We conclude with a suggested organizational model that supports an effective youthful offender program and supports the several concepts we already have articulated.

Administrative Models

The first historical references to organizational and administrative principles come from China (165 BC), where officials were chosen by examination, and appointments made by an established process. It was not until after the French Revolution in 1789, when Max Weber first posited the ideal organization and coined the term, *bureaucracy*, that organizational processes actually were formalized. Weber first identified the five fundamental principles integral to any organizational bureaucracy. These included: 1) a division of tasks; 2) hierarchical structures; 3) a formal set of rules; 4) impersonality between superiors, subordinates, and their clients; and 5) employment for life with promotion by merit. Since that time, little has been added to these basic tenets, although many have written in this area, contributing to a large body of literature (Fayol, 1949; Gullick, 1943; Taylor, 1975; Urwick, 1955, 1961).

Within the justice systems, and the juvenile justice systems in particular, three management and organizational clusters have evolved. The first is the chain-of-command theories, which structure administration in a hierarchical fashion, in that formal authority as well as communication flows from the top of the system to the bottom. Decisions are made by those at the top (or close to the top) of the organization, and those at or near the bottom of the administrative structure are expected to implement the decisions that are made.

Advantages in adopting the chain-of-command management structures include: a) the ability to make decisions and mandate actions with little debate and resistance; b) the ability to make decisions quickly without much need for consultation and collaboration; and c) the ability to enforce decisions that require one-way communication. Personnel who work in this type of structure spend a great deal of time and effort exercising control over those below them in the hierarchical structure. They also spend an equal or greater amount of time protecting themselves from those above them in the same chain-of-command structure. In youthful offender systems, youths as clients often are perceived, and in reality are, at the bottom of the hierarchy with the least formal authority. As such, they require the most effort to control.

The second group of management theories that has evolved is referred to as parent-child management theories. In organizations that employ this theory, the chief executive officer (commissioner, warden, or facility director) is perceived as and behaves as the parent, while the staff within the institution are perceived as and behave as the children. There are classic examples of this structure within the juvenile systems such as (Daddy George's) George Junior Republic and (Father Flanagan's) Boys' Town. The struggle between the warden as parent figure with the staff as "children" is central to the growth and development of the programs and services within the institution under this model. The administrative model reflects the same pattern that exists between the staff and the youths they serve. Staff and youths are viewed as growing and developing through stages of development. Administrative organizations that endorse this administrative structure assume that everyone—children, staff, and administrators—is human with essentially the same feelings, needs, and interpersonal actions. All are on a continuum of development and growth, and so human interactions are a priority and are emphasized in this kind of an organization.

Developmental-community theories are the third cluster of organizational theories, and assume social interaction as an integral part of the operation of the system. Those who endorse these administrative practices advocate for the creation of an environment that supports personal and professional growth. In this approach, there is a direct positive relationship between the level to which the individual within the organization feels protected, emotionally supported, recognized, and valued, and the individual's ability to function as part of an integrated social group that increases the competency of the structure to plan, solve problems, and make decisions. In essence, it is a human support system that is capable of responding to the individuals within it, and provides what is needed to accomplish the mission, goals, and objectives of the institution. Chart 3.4 (pages 76-82) provides a comparison of management issues across the three theoretical management clusters we have described.

Chart 3.4: Comparison of Management Issues

I. Task Performance

A. Responsibility for Execution of Task

Chain-of-Command Model:	Parent-Child Model:	Developmental Community Model:
Task responsibility is distributed among several departments and persons.	Almost complete responsibility for task execution is in the hands of the workers.	Task execution is monitored by the appropriate support group or decision center.

B. Workers' Time

Chain-of-Command Model:	Parent-Child Model:	Developmental Community Model:
Personnel work on a standard eight-hour day; a sharp distinction is made between on-the-job time and off-the-job time.	Most of the workers' time is given over to caring for the clients; no sharp distinction is made between on-the-job time and off-the job time.	Workers' time is divided between working with clients and working with fellow staff members in the support group or decision center processes. Distinction is made between on-the-job time and off-the job time since a shift system is used. Much voluntary time is given to informal processes. One measure of the success of the support system is how much extra time is spent in an informal process.

C. Continuity of Treatment

Chain-of-Command Model:	Parent-Child Model:	Developmental Community Model:
Different persons pace the client through different aspects and phases.	One person is with the client through all phases.	Continuity of treatment comes through a detailed developmental plan for growth. All staff members relate to and contribute to this plan.

Chart 3.4: Comparison of Management Issues (con't)

D. Worker Autonomy

Chain-of-Command Model:	Parent-Child Model:	Developmental Community Model:
The worker has little autonomy in the execution of the task.	The worker has complete autonomy in the execution of the task.	The autonomy of the worker is modified by the client's developmental plan, which is jointly developed by the staff. Each support team has a specific task in developing the overall plan and monitors the individual worker's performance.

II. Worker's Personality

A. Worker's Inner Needs

Chain-of-Command Model:	Parent-Child Model:	Developmental Community Model:
Inner needs are masked under routine and frozen professional competence. Unless directly related to the task at hand, they have no legitimate place here.	The large energy output drawn from inner needs is accepted and used.	A worker's needs or motives reflect structural aspects of his or her development, which is evaluated by the worker and the appropriate support group. As the support group helps make the worker aware of needs and helps to meet some of them, the emphasis shifts away from the clients having to meet the worker's needs. (It is recognized that unless the clients satisfy certain staff needs, the workers will not stay in this field very long.)

Chart 3.4: Comparison of Management Issues (con't)

B. Resolution of Worker's Own Problems

Chain-of-Command Model:	Parent-Child Model:	Developmental Community Model:
The worker seeking resolution of his or her own problems by working with clients is not desired. Resources outside the workplace are to be used.	The worker seeks solutions for his or her own problems through work with the children, or through advice from the directors.	The worker gets help from his or her support group for the solution of his or her own problems as they arise.

C. Possessiveness of Client

Chain-of-Command Model:	Parent-Child Model:	Developmental Community Model:
Possessiveness is considered an obstacle to work.	The worker is possessive of the client.	The question of individual possessiveness of the client is raised and discussed. The main goal is to have the support group care about the client in a deep way.

D. Worker's Involvement with Clients

Chain-of-Command Model:	Parent-Child Model:	Developmental Community Model:
Deep involvement of the worker with the client is an obstacle to the efficient functioning of the system.	The worker is deeply involved with the client.	The worker's personal involvement is directed towards involvement in the support group process that is going on with the clients.

E. Gratification of Worker's Primary Narcissistic Needs

Chain-of-Command Model:	Parent-Child Model:	Developmental Community Model:
Such seeking of gratification is not desirable.	The worker gratifies narcissistic needs in task performance.	Primary gratification comes from the worker's total function—working with clients and fellow members of his or her support group and his or her overall identification with the agency.

Chart 3.4: Comparison of Management Issues (con't)

III. The Director

A. Authority

Chain-of-Command Model:	Parent-Child Model:	Developmental Community Model:
Department head.	Overall director.	Support group facilitator or decision center manager (titles are interchangeable).

B. Staff Relationship to Authority

Chain-of-Command Model:	Parent-Child Model:	Developmental Community Model:
The staff is subordinate.	The director is limited by staff autonomy.	The director has a sphere of influence through his or her administrative support group whose specific functions are separate from management functions. The other support groups have specific functions (management, clinical, child care, school, aftercare, and so forth) and are autonomous, although each group has members which overlap into other support groups and other functions.

C. Decision Making

Chain-of-Command Model:	Parent-Child Model:	Developmental Community Model:
Person governs by "policy decision."	Director permits staff autonomy.	Decision making is done in each functional support group or "decision center" (the terms are interchangeable).

Chart 3.4: Comparison of Management Issues (con't)

D. Responsibility

Chain-of-Command Model:	Parent-Child Model:	Developmental Community Model:
Person's responsibility is only for the departmental task.	Responsibility, since it is for the total task, is heavy and oppressive.	The decision centers share responsibility for the total agency.

E. Relationship to Agency Operations

Chain-of-Command Model:	Parent-Child Model:	Developmental Community Model:
Person tends to be distant, even from departmental operations, because of delegation of tasks to executive officers.	Director is close to all operations.	None of the decision center managers or support group facilitators can distance themselves from the group's operation.

F. Dependence on Individuals

Chain-of-Command Model:	Parent-Child Model:	Developmental Community Model:
Dependence varies.	The director is heavily dependent on autonomous workers because of the difficulty in replacing their complex training.	The decision center manager (support group facilitator) depends on the strength of his or her support group process. If it is strong, then loss of individual members and the incorporation of new ones can proceed fairly smoothly. If the support process is weak, then the loss of individuals is disruptive.

Chart 3.4: Comparison of Management Issues (con't)

G. In-service Training

Chain-of-Command Model:	Parent-Child Model:	Developmental Community Model:
Responsibility for training is delegated, with a resulting increase in social distance between the worker and the department head.	Responsibility for in-service training cannot be delegated.	In-service training for the support group is developed by the group and probably led by the facilitator. Overall training for individual agency members in the cognitive-structural developmental theory and practice is handled by the in-service training programs.

H. Involvement with Workers

Chain-of-Command Model:	Parent-Child Model:	Developmental Community Model:
There is little involvement of the department head with the workers.	There is a deep mutual involvement of directors and workers.	The support group process cannot succeed unless the group facilitator is deeply involved.

I. Vertical Distance Between Directors and Workers

Chain-of-Command Model:	Parent-Child Model:	Developmental Community Model:
There is a maximization of vertical distance and a conscious emphasis on "equality" as a stress-reducing technique. (True equality is obtained, by and large, only within each echelon.)	There is a diminution of vertical distance between the director and workers, and an ethos of equality.	Unless there is an equality of spirit in the sharing of selves, the support group cannot work.

Chart 3.4: Comparison of Management Issues (con't)

IV. The Clients

A. Separation of Client System and Worker System

Chain-of-Command Model:	Parent-Child Model:	Developmental Community Model:
The two systems are strictly separated.	There is a diminution of separation between the client system and the worker system.	The client system is structurally the same as the worker system and they overlap.

B. Internalization of Client by Worker

Chain-of-Command Model:	Parent-Child Model:	Developmental Community Model:
Internalization of the client by the worker does not occur.	The client is internalized by the worker.	The client's support group is internalized by the worker. The worker also has to internalize his or her own staff support process.

C. Status of the Worker

Chain-of-Command Model:	Parent-Child Model:	Developmental Community Model:
Status of the worker is dependent on his or her relative detachment from the client.	Status of the worker is dependent on his or her involvement in the client.	Worker status depends on involvement with the client's support group and involvement with his or her own group.

Situational Leadership

Hersey and Blanchard (1977) posited a theory of leadership that many believe is helpful to administrators, especially those who espouse prescriptive programming for youthful offenders. Using the principles of situational leadership, managers are able to assess and diagnose the particular attributes of a given situation in order to choose the most appropriate management style to foster worker productivity and growth.

According to Hersey and Blanchard's theory, juvenile institutional managers who adopt situational leadership as their organizational structure have the opportunity to determine the amount of task behavior (direction) and the amount of relationship behavior (socio-emotional support) necessary to furnish or cater to staff, given the situation and the level of maturity of the staff. They define task behavior as the extent to which a leader engages in one-way communication by explaining what each follower is to do as well as when, where, and how tasks are to be accomplished.

They define relationship behavior as the extent to which a leader engages in two-way communication by providing socio-emotional support, "psychological strokes," and facilitating behaviors. The maturity level of a worker is defined as a combination of his or her ability and willingness to take responsibility as well as education, experience, and the capacity to set high and achievable goals.

Hersey and Blanchard suggest that a manager's style may be plotted on a two-dimensional axis, and leadership style may be depicted in one of four ways as shown in Chart 3.5 (page 84). Situational leadership, as a management tool, is an interaction among the amount of task behavior and relationship behavior a supervisor (manager) displays towards a worker in a given situation and the worker's maturity level exhibited on certain tasks. As the level of maturity of the subordinate increases, given a specific task assignment, the manager needs to reduce the amount of task behavior and increase the amount of relationship behavior exhibited. As the subordinate develops beyond the average level of maturity and is able to function more independently, given the assigned task, the manager needs to decrease both task behaviors and relationship behaviors relative to leadership styles.

As the subordinate is able to provide his or her own socio-emotional support, the manager needs to reinforce this type of behavior and dependency with decreasing frequency. Thus, there is less supervision and greater delegation of responsibility, given a specific task situation. It is the appropriate leadership styles of the manager, given the maturity of the subordinate worker in any given task situation, that makes situational leadership a most potent management and supervisory tool for the youthful offender administrator.

Chart 3.5 — Supervisor's/Manager's Style

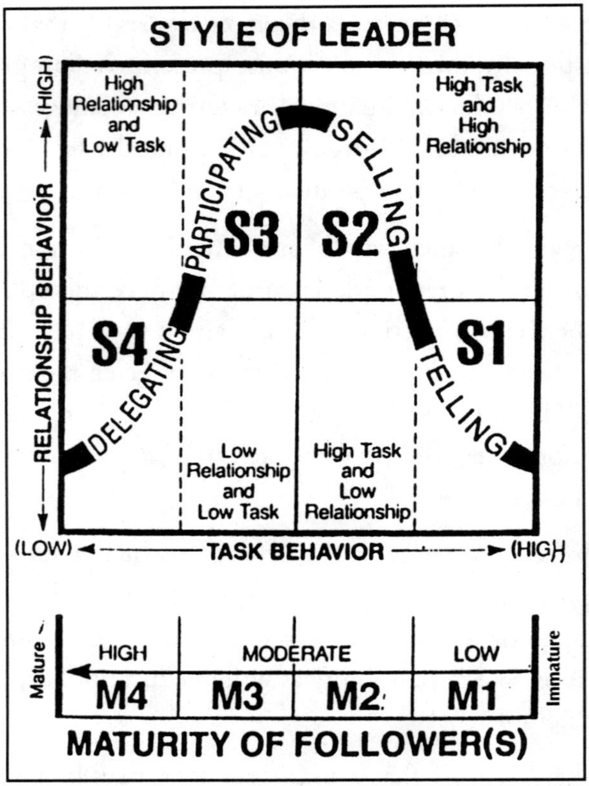

As shown in Chart 3.5 (above), a supervisor/manager's style is dependent on the maturity level of the subordinate. That includes the amount of direction the worker requires and the amount of socio-emotional support the manager must provide. Generally speaking, those workers who are low in maturity (M1), given a specific task, have the highest probability of success in that task if their supervisor provides high-task and low-relationship managerial behaviors (S1). Those workers who are low-to-moderate in their maturity levels (M2) will experience the highest degree of success if their supervisors demonstrate high-task and high-relationship behaviors in their management style (S2). Those workers who are moderate to high in maturity level (M3) will benefit most from managers and supervisors who provide high-relationship and low-task supervisory behaviors (S3).

Finally, workers who are of the highest maturity level (M4) given a particular task, require managers who provide low-task and low-relationship behaviors. The four leadership styles that emerge from situational leadership theory are telling, selling, participating, and delegating. They are described in greater detail when we introduce the youth development system later in this section.

We consider situational leadership to have wide application for the youthful offenders. It is easily administered within an institution, no matter what the size of the organization.

Although Hersey has modified the language in subsequent iterations (we believe this original version is easier and simpler to use), technology and instrumentation have been developed to help managers assess the leadership styles of all personnel. We now turn to a participatory management structure that integrates the various administrative and organizational principles we have introduced thus far.

COMMUNITY DECISION CENTER ORGANIZATIONS

The fundamental premise of this management approach, first developed in Michigan and used in several juvenile justice institutions since 1973, is to design a management supervisory system that integrates the various complex components that also are in youthful offender programs. Such programs and services as housing, education, vocational and occupational programs, recreation, behavioral management, counseling, administration of critical incidents (use of force), and case management are often discreet entities within the institution and have little or no coordination. Youthful offender programs sometimes are a nightmare to manage, yet the community-decision center organizational structure supports the integration of supervisory and treatment components that operate within the corrections system mandated to provide services to youthful offenders.

The community decision center model is basically people oriented. It assumes that people are basically good and desire to perform successfully at their jobs. Central to the model is the assertion that participatory management within the institution is preferable to decisions made by one or a few. It also declares that responsibility may be delegated to mature workers with the authority to accomplish tasks and the accountability mechanisms to insure successful accomplishment of assignments. Finally, the model allows for the planning and decision-making processes to occur using individuals within the organization to support each other when meeting problems, identifying issues, and deciding actions. We offer several operational definitions to effect the model:

- A manager is one who creates the environment in which staff can grow and develop both personally and professionally.
- A supervisor is one who monitors staff tasks, sets standards for work to be accomplished, provides feedback to employees to help them alter their behaviors and learn new ones, trains staff on skills required to accomplish their tasks, and is an advocate for their staff.
- The decision center is the basic structure within the community development center model.

It is incumbent on the manager and the supervisor to maximize staff potential. Only then can the various components of the youthful offender program within the institution be integrated into a holistic unit that is perceived by offenders as organized, consistent, safe, and predictable. The decision center is a support group composed of staff with similar functions or roles within the organization. A manager who acts as the link among the other managers of the institution chairs these decision centers. There are as many decision centers as there are major functions within the institution. Depending on the size of the system, some functions may be merged into one decision center. At a sixty-bed youthful offender program, for example, it is conceivable to have decision centers for education and other programs, physical plant, health and food services, fiscal and clerical operations, besides one for administration. Each decision center is managed by the most senior person available within that particular discipline.

There is, however, a wide spectrum of salary grades, educational levels, and competencies in any one decision center. The product is a cross-section of workers participating together in the administration, decision making, planning, training, and implementating of the total program. While the one disadvantage to this model is that it requires a rather confident and trusting chief executive officer (warden), the advantages that accrue, given the mission and goals of the juvenile justice system, are far reaching. Chart 3.6 represents an organizational structure that depicts a community developmental administrative model.

Chart 3.6 — Community Development Administrative Model

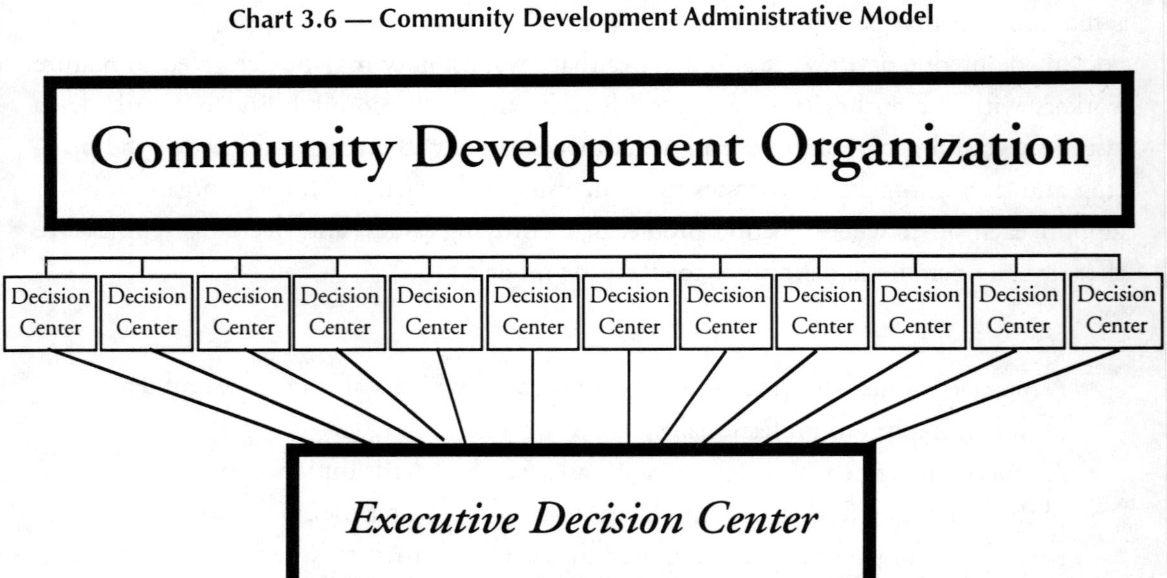

Notice that the organizational structure is not hierarchical, but circular. Each manager of a decision center has neither more nor less authority than another on the decision-making process or on managing his or her delegated responsibilities. This includes the chief executive officer (commissioner or warden) of the system, as well. Although the chief administrator is responsible for the institution or system, many of the decision-making processes are delegated to the decision centers and, in turn, use the interactions of the system already described. There are few administrative issues, such as contractual agreements or agency policies, that contradict the operations of this model. Practically, it requires relearning on the part of employees under this managerial system to behave and respond to many individuals rather than just one central figure.

The decisions that are made are shared rather than unilateral, and managers of decision centers are not merely representatives of their particular cohesive interest group, but more importantly, they are a composite of the entire system. Thus, as decision centers deliberate their problems, issues, and tasks, each becomes more aware of the other's mission, goals, and objectives. Decisions evolve and develop, broadened by the interactions between and among decision centers, influenced by the dynamics of the institutional community, and refined by the shared information that is fostered by the process. It is a management system of inclusion, rather than exclusion. It is a system of participation rather than isolation, one that implements effective and efficient organizational decisions, rather than unilateral, top-down directives. The community development model is very similar to the unit management organizational structure that has been adopted in many adult corrections systems. *See also* Levinson (1999) *Unit Management in Prisons and Jails.*

Framework for Action: The Youth Development System

We have described elsewhere (Glick, and Sturgeon, 1998) the adolescent development model and its importance for successfully implementing a youthful offender program. Staff who are able to comprehend the concepts of adolescent development and successfully apply them to the daily operations of their jobs will encounter less difficulty when managing youthful offender behavior and more satisfaction in completing assigned tasks. We often have stated that understanding adolescent development is the cornerstone of successful programming and is fundamental to reducing recidivism among young offenders (Glick and Goldstein, 1995; Glick and Sturgeon, 1998). Gaining utility with this model and applying its principles to specific functions within a youthful offender program is a skill that needs to be developed among staff. We now turn to one application of this concept and its ensuing principles as we describe the second framework for action when managing and implementing an effective youthful offender program.

Popular among youth offender programs is an applied behavior modification principle commonly referred to as "the level system." This class of behavior management tools is based on a token economy, a behavior modification theory using reinforcements, usually points, in which the young offender is rewarded for good behavior or penalized for bad behavior. Points are given when a young offender meets certain standards of behavior or demonstrates positive behavior, and points are taken away if the offender fails to meet the criterion behavior or acts inappropriately. Based upon point accumulation, offenders either may advance in level, and hence earn greater rewards, or maintain their status within their program. Sometimes, if the youthful offenders behave extraordinarily inappropriately or are perceived as regressing in behavior, they are punished with the ultimate negative reinforcement, which is to have their level in the program reduced.

Behavior modification approaches were first applied to severely developmentally delayed populations (Brown, 1991) in an attempt to train them in rather rote behavioral responses (for example, feeding themselves, buttoning clothes, learning to speak). This approach was first applied in the juvenile justice area in the 1950s and 1960s. While these approaches have been shown to be successful in modifying immediate behaviors of youths within juvenile justice programs, there is little evidence that there is a transfer of learning that occurs beyond the immediate environment in which it is practiced. Certainly, there is little evidence that the techniques are based on adolescent development or that they incorporate the technology and theory we have espoused.

Youth Development System

We offer as an alternative for behavior management within the youthful offender programs, a youth development system that is based on adolescent development principles. When applying adolescent development to a youth behavior management system, there is an expectation that skills are learned and responsibilities are acquired as youthful offenders increase in their development and master the developmental skills associated with the four domains in the adolescent development model (physical, cognitive, social, and emotional). As such, privileges given to the youthful offender are based on their demonstrated level of responsibility (as defined by the program) rather than the number of points they have earned. Unlike their adult offender counterparts, youths are presumed to be skill-deficient and hence begin with few rewards or privileges, but earn them as they learn, grow, and develop through their adolescence.

The youth development system is rather simple to design and administer. Typically, four stages are identified. The stages are progressive and consecutive, which means that one stage builds on the other, and youthful offenders cannot advance unless they have demonstrated specific responsibilities and certain skill competencies associated with a particular stage. Once a young person has earned a specific stage, as certified by staff, that stage cannot be taken away. Herein lies a basic difference between a youth development system based on adolescent development concepts and a level system based on behavior modification theory.

Once staff certify that a youthful offender has acquired a set of responsibilities and cognitive skills as identified by the program for that discreet stage in the youth development system, staff cannot punish that youth for inappropriate program behavior by taking the level from that offending youth. The youth development system does hold youths accountable for inappropriate behavior or rule violations; however, it does so within a learning context, where all situations are used as experiences to teach skills and responsibilities to the offender.

When designing the youth development system, one needs to be familiar with the adolescent development model (Glick, and Sturgeon, 1998) and comprehend those principles using youth offender situations. Once staff has utility in applying the adolescent development principles, one must decide the number of stages that should be incorporated into the youth development system.

Commonly, there are four stages in the youth development system; however, some systems have as many as six stages. Staff first should identify the skills and responsibilities that the youthful offender will acquire as a result of participating in the program. Then, staff need to identify all the incentives (rewards) that are available to the youthful offender while in the program. Once these lists have been generated, staff need to put each list in order using the principles of the adolescent development model, assigning skills and responsibilities to each stage and matching rewards to the listed responsibilities.

The youth development system model that is presented here has been developed over a twenty-five-year period, first at a private child care agency for emotionally disturbed, delinquent adolescents (1970), and then at several New York State Division for Youth Facilities (1976). Many individuals have worked on its development and added to the richness of the model, until the present where it is currently being used systemwide in a number of jurisdictions. These include the New York State Office of Children and Family Services Residential Centers, the State of Louisiana Department of Public Safety, and the Colorado Department of Corrections Youth Offender System, to name but a few. All, however, are based on the adolescent development model and its underlying principles that we have described.

Staff

Underpinning the youth development system is the staff who implement it. Staff constantly must adjust their behavior based on the youthful offender's stage within the youth development system and the particular, current situation. These interactions are based on Hersey and Blanchard's (1977, 1985) concepts of situational leadership (discussed elsewhere in this section).

As depicted in Chart 3.7, (on page 91), information about the youthful offenders is provided for each of the four stages. The following data should be detailed: specific beliefs and thoughts about placement; the youthful offenders' cognitive skill levels; the motivation and confidence levels towards self and others; the youthful offenders' attitudes and behaviors; the responsibility the youthful offenders take for their own behavior (internal versus external locus of control); and their leadership abilities. The staff's interaction style is then prescriptively matched with the youths' stages within the youth development system. The staff interaction styles include the following:

Telling: Staff direct youthful offenders, telling them what to do, when to do it, and specifically how to complete a task. Staff do not yell, but control youthful offender behavior and activity. Telling means stating things in a concrete, consistent, and objective manner. In this stage, staff maintains close and constant supervision of the young offenders.

Selling: Staff, using this style, still maintain close supervision, directing, and telling the youth in a consistent and firm manner, what to do, when to do it, and suggesting how to accomplish the task. Unlike the first stage, staff offer advice, provide explanations and reasons for doing a task a certain way, and request some feedback from the youthful offenders as they complete their responsibilities. Staff provide encouragement and support to the youthful offenders to help them accept responsibility for their actions.

Participating: Youthful offenders at stage three have demonstrated more responsibility for their actions and the decisions they make. They even accept more initiative for their own goals and objectives as stated in their case management plans. Staff, in turn, use a highly supportive style for youthful offenders as they attempt to resolve problems. They offer direction to the offenders on an as-needed basis, but staff offer advice only as it is related to the offender's progress in their program. Staff encourage youth to set their own goals and begin to plan for their future (whether it be on release to the community or into the general population).

Delegating: At the final stage in the youthful offender system, staff provide offenders with minimal direction as they complete their program. At this stage, youthful offenders demonstrate proficiency in completing their assignments with responsibility and independence. Staff do not need to provide close supervision and may allow youthful offenders latitude and flexibility within the limits of the institutional policies and procedures. The staff is still the authority and needs to constantly reinforce this as they provide more opportunities for the youthful offender to explore, especially in the later stages of their adolescent development where independence and self-directedness become important.

Chart 3.7: Youth Development System Elements

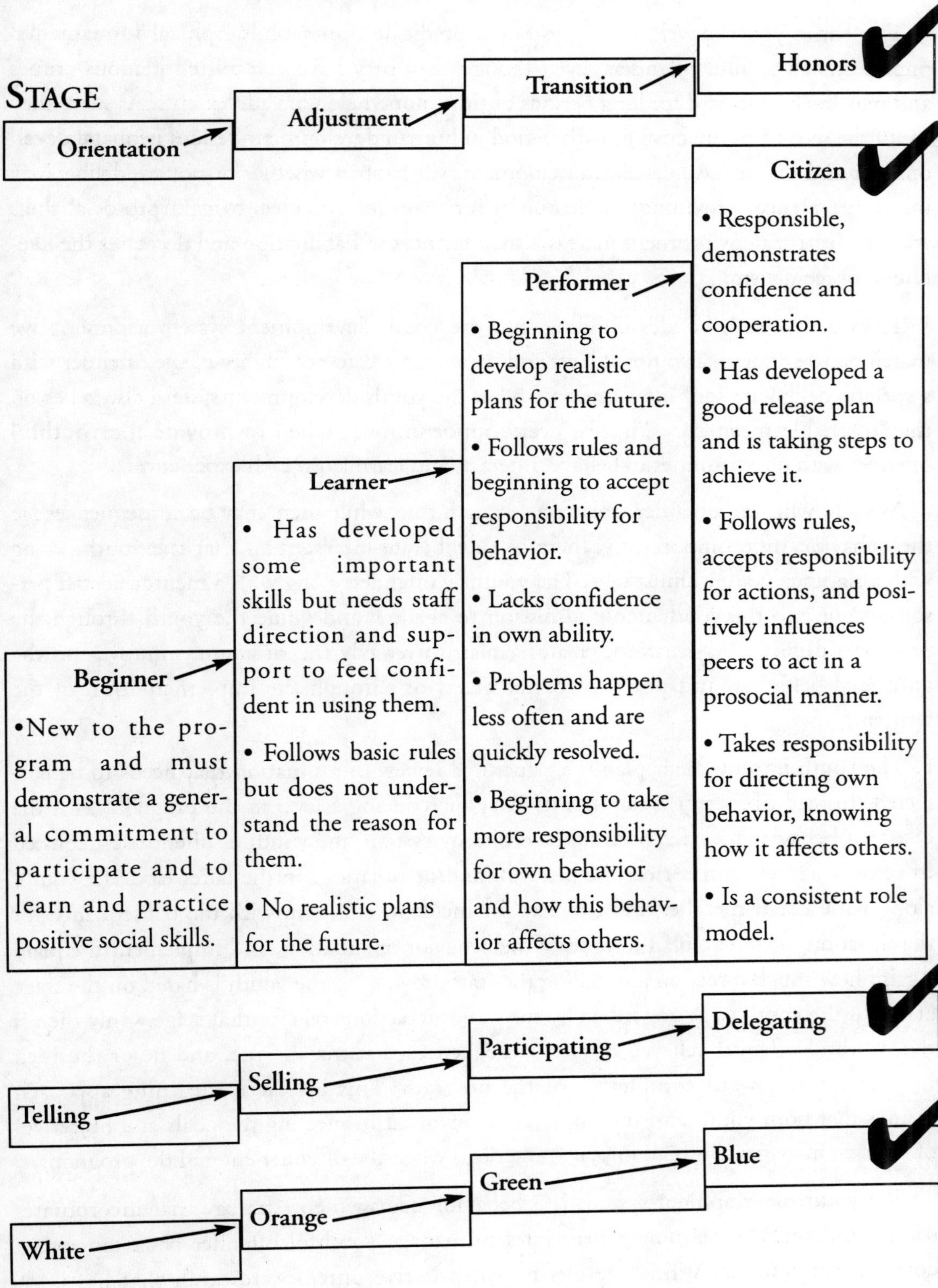

Youth Are Still Adolescents

The entire youth development system is predicated on a philosophical fundamental premise that youthful offenders, even though they may have committed heinous crimes and may be incarcerated for long periods of time, nonetheless are adolescents. As such, they are in the second most active growth period in human development besides neonatal development and infancy. Adolescent development will happen whether or not we deliberately intervene. Hence, providing opportunities for youthful offenders to gain prosocial skills within a learning environment increases their chances of habilitation and decreases the likelihood of recidivism.

Toward that end, besides building into the youth development system a prescriptive match between the maturational level and demonstrated responsibility of the offender with a specific deliberate staff intervention (style), the youth development system also relies on the "teachable moment." That is, every opportunity is taken to provide the youthful offender with opportunities to behave, interact, and learn from each experience.

As such, when an offender violates a program rule, while there may be consequences for the behavior, more importantly, there is a deliberate intervention that the youth, along with a significant adult, must take. The youthful offender, along with a mentor (a staff person assigned to the youth upon admission to shadow and guide the youth through the program) dissects the situation, creates a plan to remedy the situation, improves on the antisocial behavior, and practices better behavior through the implementation of the written plan.

The youth improvement plan is a structured review of a situation that needs to be corrected. Instead of merely taking points away or reducing a level in the program, as is the case in a behavior modification, token-economy system, the youthful offender is required to actively address and correct the behavior and/or situation. In the latter case, the youth, along with a staff member, must review the incident, come up with the consequence for the situation, prepare a plan to modify the behavior or situation, and implement the plan. Again, how much direction and telling the staff provides to the youth is based on the stage at which the youth is, as prescribed by the staff interaction style for that stage. Only then is the youthful offender relieved of any consequences that may accrue, and he or she then may continue toward completion of the program. This interactive learning approach insures that both youth and staff are actively involved in meeting the goals and objectives of the case management plan initially prescribed when the offender entered the program.

The youth development system is a behavior management strategy that incorporates sound adolescent development principles to manage youthful offender behavior within correctional systems. While there is no quantitative outcome research that has been conducted to assess its efficacy, there is a body of qualitative reports that endorse its utility in the operation of a youth offender program (American Correctional Association, *Best Practices: Excellence in Corrections*, 1998). The overarching rationale to adopt such a model is that it does the following:

- Provides staff with concrete tools which they can use to manage aggressive and acting-out youthful offender behavior
- Provides young offenders with competencies, skills, and alternatives to use when dealing with their daily experiences
- Enhances opportunities to problem solve in potentially antisocial and negative situations
- Encourages development of responsible behavior based on adolescent development concepts
- Reduces subjective applications of rewards and punishments
- Standardizes program operations for staff and youthful offenders
- Focuses learning and applications on youth developmental tasks

In this section, we have provided the frameworks for action based on those mechanisms that staff may use to implement effective and efficient programs for youthful offenders placed in adult correctional systems. We have attempted to present these in a manner that helps integrate and ultimately synthesize an approach to deal with youthful offenders placed in adult justice systems. Taken together, these frameworks for action provide readers with the tools necessary to organize the system's environment, manage its workforce, and supervise its youth population with minimal untoward incidents. The techniques shared here are examples of a class of interventions we encourage the readers to understand and apply to their own unique situations.

Chapter 4

The How To's and What If's

Introduction

Ready, get set, go! We have finished describing the planning, design, and development phases of the youthful offender program, and now you should be ready to implement it. The purpose of this section is to provide some fundamental operational tactics to deal with the start-up and ongoing maintenance of the program. We have collected much of this information from our experience operating programs for youthful offenders and have used ideas provided to us as we have visited throughout various corrections systems. We provide a variety of ideas which you may choose to use directly, or perhaps alter to meet your own circumstance. Whatever the case, we encourage you to think beyond the comfort zones of your traditional paradigms. Think multidimensionally as you approach some of these basic issues.

Policy Direction and Approvals

Once the legislative and executive branches of government have determined that youths under the criminal age of majority will be treated and housed as adults, the state agency mandated to implement the statute must set policy direction and gain support for the program. As such, the chief executive officer of the agency must be able to garner support from colleagues, staff, professional organizations, and stakeholders. We have stated elsewhere (Glick and Sturgeon, 1998) that the process of designing, developing, and implementing a youthful offender program is arduous and requires precision and deliberate, definitive action. The policy team convened and directed by the chief executive officer of the agency must include the agency's executive staff, wardens, and support personnel. This section includes a series of strategies to accomplish this task. This chapter is based on the questions we have encountered. We thought that this question and answer format would permit you to learn from the experience of others.

As chief executive officer of the agency, what is the most efficient means to monitor the progress of the design, development, and implementation of the youthful offender program?

Several mechanisms should be used to monitor progress and program efficiency. First, weekly executive staff meetings allow staff to receive updates from the administrator charged with direct oversight of the program. These verbal reports should be specific relative to the following:

- Progress of the project since the last report
- Status report, given the approved management and implementation plan
- Difficulties and/or barriers encountered that require the chief executive officer's attention
- Problems encountered and solutions implemented

Second, the chief executive officer should have a checklist similar to the following one that provides written documentation of progress. Complete the checklist at least monthly until the program is fully implemented.

CHECKLIST FOR AGENCY HEADS

1. Has the mission of the program been approved? Yes _ No _
See Chapter 2 for a definition of a mission statement and the process necessary to develop one.

2. Have the goals and objectives for the program been approved? Yes _ No _
Goals Statement(s): (Be sure each goal is listed clearly.)

3. Has a person been identified and charged with the responsibility to develop and implement the program? Yes _ No _
Name: ______________________________ **Title:** ______________________________
(There has to be a single person identified who is responsible to ensure that the project stays on track and that it conforms with its established goals and objectives.)

4. Has a timeline been established for the development and implementation of the program? Yes _ No _
(See Chapter 2 for the definition of and process for the development of timelines. The importance of time lines often is underestimated and overlooked. Yet, the timeline is what helps the manager keep the project on track.)

5. Has a clear reporting chain been established? Yes _ No _
(See Chapter 2 for responsibility charting and the communications process. See Chapter 3 on administrative models of the organization.)

6. Do members of the executive staff know their role in the development and implementation of the program? Yes _ No _
The successful youthful offender program requires the entire executive staff to know exactly what they are responsible for and to demonstrate their support for the youthful offender program. ! ithout this commitment, the development and implementation of the program could experience numerous delays.

7. Are the stakeholders well informed and do they receive routine communications?
Yes _ No _

8. Have the stakeholders received a packet of information that contains the following? Yes _ No _

_ The program's goals and objectives

_ Programmatic components

_ Duration of each segment

_ Criteria for selection into the program

9. Is the public information officer familiar with the mission, goals, objectives, and operational details of the program? Yes _ No _

10. Is there adequate funding for the first year of the program? Yes _ No _

11. Is the program carefully monitored for at least the first six months?
The first six months of any youthful offender program can be, and usually are, very challenging. These challenges can manifest themselves as:

- Staff turnover and staff replacement
- Replacement staff not trained on how to manage youthful offenders
- Changes in the daily schedule
- Changes in the programmatic elements of the program
- Unnecessary spending (to maintain cost efficiencies)
- Program straying from its goals and objectives (in other words, it becomes too punitive or it becomes too lax)

There are three reasons for this type of fluctuation in the program:

- The staff is unfamiliar with their roles and do not understand how the program is supposed to operate.
- The staff is unfamiliar with how to manage youthful offenders. Some staff have unreasonable expectations of youthful offenders and/or the youthful offender program. Usually the staff has some orientation and preservice training; however, it still takes about a month of on-the-job experience to apply much of this new knowledge and skill.

- The youthful offenders are unfamiliar with what is expected of them. Our experience shows that youthful offenders who have spent a great deal of time in the adult prison environment will have the greatest difficulty adjusting to a youthful offender program.

12. Does the program administrator meet with those responsible for the operation of the program at least monthly for the first year? Yes _ No _

The "direct" involvement of the agency's executive with those responsible for the implementation and operation of the youthful offender program is critical to its successful operation. Unlike other "new" programs, a youthful offender program is so unique to the operation of an adult corrections system, that it demands the attention of the agency executive. The chief executive officer should communicate with the various stakeholders interested in the corrections system's programs and the youthful offender program. The following are examples of letters that the chief executive officer may wish to send to individuals. Sometimes, it is preferable for the warden of the facility that will house the youthful offender program to send these letters personally.

<u>*Letter to Executive Branch Politicians*</u>

Dear Executive *(Town Supervisor, County Executive, and the like—use their specific name and title)*:

The Department of Corrections is implementing a program for juvenile offenders who have been adjudicated as adults and have been sentenced by the courts to the department. As you know, placing youthful offenders in adult systems provides different challenges for our corrections systems. As such, I wish to advise you of several issues and actions that we are taking in order for us to continue to serve your constituency well, while continuing to meet our agency mandate.

The youthful offender program is designed around, and is based on, the most effective correctional practices and well-researched interventions. Our program model acknowledges that these young offenders, while having committed serious crimes, are still in an active growth period, and so much of what we do is based on sound adolescent development theory. We also insure that we meet the requirements of statutes, regulations, and agency policies.

The program is highly structured and demands that the youthful offenders be active participants with the staff in the program. The youthful offender program is designed to last (*fill in its duration*). At its conclusion, the youthful offenders either will be paroled or moved into the general inmate population. The Department has decided to locate the youthful offenders at (*insert name of institution(s)*), which is/are located in your constituent community.

To best meet the developmental needs of the youthful offenders, we shall offer a variety of programs and services. Some of these are mandated by law, others by regulation, and still others by our position that these youthful offenders will be returning to their communities, and we want them to be prepared to be constructive citizens. The program components include but are not limited to: (*Each department will have to fill in its own program components but should include as examples: education, vocational training, Aggression Replacement Training, recreation, and counseling, to name but a few*).

Because we are committed to the mission and goals of the youthful offender program, we have trained our staff in the following specific areas:

- adolescent development
- cognitive-behavioral approaches to change youthful offender behavior
- behavior management
- security issues
- special needs

I have enclosed a detailed description of the program including its mission, goals, objectives, and daily activity schedule. From time to time, I shall send you program updates. If you have any questions, please do not hesitate to contact me at (*provide your direct office number*).

Sincerely,

<u>LETTER TO LEGISLATORS, POLITICIANS</u>

Dear (*use full name with correct title, for example, Assemblyman, Senator, Congresswoman, Alderman*):

As you know, recently passed legislation requires the Department of Corrections to provide programs for youthful offenders, who are youths under the age of criminal responsibility, who have been adjudicated as adults and placed within the adult corrections system.

Placing youthful offenders in adult systems provides different challenges for our corrections systems. As such, I wish to advise you of several issues and actions that we are taking for us to continue to serve your constituency well, while continuing to meet our agency mandate.

The youthful offender program is designed around, and is based on, the most effective correctional practices and well-researched interventions. Our program model acknowledges that these young offenders, while having committed serious crimes, are still in an active growth period, and so much of what we do is based on sound adolescent development theory. Additionally, we insure that we meet the requirements of statutes, regulations, and agency policies.

The program is highly structured and demands that the youthful offenders be active participants with the staff in the program. The youthful offender program is designed to last (*fill in its duration*). At its conclusion, the youthful offenders either will be paroled or moved into the general inmate population. The Department has decided to place the youthful offenders at (*insert name of institution(s)*), which is/are located in your legislative district.

To best meet the developmental needs of the youthful offenders, we shall offer a variety of programs and services. Some of these are mandated by law, others by regulation, and still others by our position that these youthful offenders will be returning to their communities, and we want them to be prepared to be constructive citizens. The program components include but are not limited to: (*Each department will have to fill in its own program components but should include as examples: education, vocational training, Aggression Replacement Training, recreation, and counseling, to name but a few*).

Because we are committed to the mission and goals of the youthful offender program, we have trained our staff in the following specific areas:

- adolescent development
- cognitive-behavioral approaches to change youthful offender behavior
- behavior management
- security issues
- special needs

I have enclosed a detailed description of the program including its mission, goals, objectives, and daily activity schedule. From time to time, I shall send you program updates. If you have any questions, please do not hesitate to contact me at (*provide your direct office number*).

Sincerely,

<u>LETTER TO THE JUDICIARY</u>

Dear Judge (*personalize name*):

As you know, recently passed legislation requires the Department of Corrections to provide programs for youthful offenders, who are youths under the age of criminal responsibility, who have been adjudicated as adults and placed within the adult corrections system.

Since your court may wish to take advantage of this new placement option, we wanted to take this opportunity to familiarize you with the program, and invite you to visit the program when your calendar permits. Since placing youthful offenders in adult systems provides different challenges for our corrections systems, I also wish to advise you of several issues and actions that we are taking to meet our agency mandates, including insuring the safety and security of the community.

The youthful offender program is based on correctional best practices and well-researched interventions. Our program model acknowledges that these young offenders, while having committed serious crimes, are still in an active growth period, and so much of what we do is based on sound adolescent development theory. We also insure that we meet the requirements of statutes, regulations, and agency policies.

The program is highly structured and demands that the youthful offenders be active participants with the staff in the program. The youthful offender program is designed to last (*fill in its duration*). At its conclusion, the youthful offenders either will be paroled or moved into the general inmate population. The Department has decided to place the youthful offenders at (*insert name of institution(s)*), which is/are located in your judicial district.

To best meet the developmental needs of the youthful offenders, we shall offer a variety of programs and services. Some of these are mandated by law, others by regulation, and still others by our position that these youthful offenders will be returning to their communities, and we want them to be prepared to be constructive citizens. The program components include but are not limited to: (*Each department will have to fill in its own program components but should include as examples: education, vocational training, Aggression Replacement Training, recreation, and counseling, to name but a few*).

Because we are committed to the mission and goals of the youthful offender program, we have trained our staff in the following specific areas:

- adolescent development
- cognitive-behavioral approaches to change youthful offender behavior
- behavior management
- security issues
- special needs

I have enclosed a detailed description of the program including its mission, goals, objectives, and daily activity schedule. From time to time, I shall send you program updates. If you have any questions, please do not hesitate to contact me at (*provide your direct office number*).

Sincerely,

Include the following:

- the program's mission statement
- the program's goals and objectives
- the daily schedule for all of the phases
- an outline of staff training

Program Direction and Operations

Once the policy direction is established and the chief executive officer has taken strategic action, the warden and the local institution in which the youthful offender program is placed must begin to administer and manage the program implementation. Many issues and questions arise that require innovative and creative responses from the institution. Some issues may be unique to the particular institution in which the youthful offender program is placed, but for the most part, certain core areas must be addressed.

I am the warden responsible for the youthful offender program. I must ensure that the youthful offender program is incorporated into the regular operations of my facility. I also am charged by the chief executive officer of the agency to insure that the youthful offender program is successful. What are the issues I must address to meet my obligations to the existing prison population and the direction from the executive?

CHECKLIST FOR FACILITY WARDENS

1. Where "exactly" in the facility will the program be housed? ______________________
   Will the program have an entire living unit? Yes _ No _
2. Will the program have to share a living unit with adult inmates? Yes _ No _
3. If the youthful offender program will be housed in a living area where adult inmates also are held, how will they be kept separated by "sight and sound"?
   For example, explain in detail:
   Inmate movement
   How showers and restroom facilities will be shared
   Dayroom schedule
   Out-of-cell schedule
   Indoor schedule
4. When "exactly" will the youthful offenders be able to use the outdoor recreation facilities?
   Identify days of the week ________________________and exact times ___________.
5. Where "exactly" will the youthful offenders' outdoor recreation occur?
   Youthful offenders need organized outdoor recreation and exercise daily. It is extremely important that the outdoor exercise for youthful offenders blends into the rest of

their programming. For example, do not schedule outdoor recreation just prior to educational activities since the recreation increases their hyperactivity, and youths tend to become overheated requiring showers and a change of clothing.

6. Identify what outdoor recreation areas will be used. ____________________.
   (Special attention is needed to prevent youthful offenders from coming into contact with adult inmates going to or coming from the recreation yard.) Ensure that the staffing pattern for recreation takes into account issues for recreational staff and security personnel.
7. In a central dining facility, when will the youthful offenders eat?
   It has been our experience that in a central dining situation, it is better to have the youthful offenders' mealtime either first or last. Also, the warden needs to ensure that the youthful offenders' dietary needs are met. It is crucial to have a significant staff presence during meals. This staff presence should include security supervisors and staff, program staff, representation from the administration, and as often as possible, the program administrator.
8. What will be the facility's reporting chain?
   Several different examples of reporting chains may be used. One includes a deputy or assistant warden who is responsible for the day-to-day operations of the program who reports daily to the warden; another is a program director/manager who is responsible for the day-to-day operations of the program and reports to either the warden or the assistant warden (who in-turn reports to the warden). Whatever method is chosen, it is important that the reporting chain be clearly identified for everyone involved. The facility's warden must be kept informed about what is happening in the program. The warden should require a weekly report that includes at least the following:

   - number of youthful offenders in the program
   - number of youthful offenders in the various phases of the program
   - number and nature of incident reports written
   - number and nature of discrepancies in the daily operational schedule
   - number of youthful offenders being housed in the special management unit
   - number and nature of use-of-force reports
   - number of youthful offenders reporting for daily sick call
   - number of youthful offenders housed in the infirmary
   - number and nature of incidents in the education area
   - discrepancies and changes in the published menus
   - transfer and/or promotion of staff out of the program
   - transfer and/or promotion of staff into the program

- number of attempted suicides—what types of interventions were used?
- number of youthful offenders (who were eligible) who received visitors.

The warden of the facility should visit the program at least twice a week. Because the program is housed in a specific facility, the warden of that facility will be held accountable for the orderly operation of the program. Staff should view the warden's visits as supportive. Likewise, they should see the administrator as a person who is involved and caring, and not merely as someone on an inspection tour. We recommend that the warden visit the program daily. This is especially important during the start-up phases of the program. Experience has shown that the warden's presence throughout the program provides assurance to the staff, provides direct observation of operations, and allows the warden to provide managerial direction and to solve problems before issues become crises.

9. Ensure that the staffing patterns complement the operational needs of the program. This is without question one of the most difficult areas to determine in any youthful offender program. Traditional adult staffing patterns have been found to be insufficient to manage youthful offenders. There are several reasons for this:

   - Youthful offenders have a propensity to act out, and sometimes, do so violently.
   - Staff is required to plan more carefully for the youth's day and may need to show the youth how to accomplish tasks or learn a particular skill. For example, recreational staff have to demonstrate (model) how to play a game; and/or staff may have to coach the youthful offenders through an activity.
   - Staff shortages can be a precursor to an incident. This particular population requires constant attention.

10. Have all emergency plans been reviewed to ensure that they include the addition of the youthful offender program? Yes _ No _
    Hostage negotiations personnel should become familiar with the adolescent stages of development.

I have prepared my institution to accept a new youthful offender program. What can I do to prepare the community and the stakeholders?

Communication is key to a successful youthful offender program. The community surrounding the institution is interested in its safety, and probably is motivated to participate when asked. Toward that end, the warden should consider developing a youthful offender advisory group composed of citizens from the community. Candidates for an institutional advisory board should include politicians, civic and business leaders, local educators, professionals within the corrections system, and neighborhood citizens. The board should be small, for instance, eight-to-twelve members. It should meet perhaps quarterly or bimonthly. The purpose of the board should be to advise the warden and to help in program design, development, and implementation. The function of the advisory board is not to be policy makers, nor are they decision makers. However, they are involved and constructively provide direction and advice. To formulate the board, the warden should do the following:

- Develop a list of potential members and share it with staff for further input.
- Consult with the institution supervisor and headquarters staff (such as the public information officer, the finance officer, and the legislative liaison) to inform them of the initiative and gain their input and support).
- Place the names in priority order using such criteria as political leadership, ability to devote time, willingness to serve and volunteer, and ability to enhance the program's implementation and refinement (for example, a university faculty person may enhance internships to embellish programs, support research and program evaluation, or provide useful academic information).
- Telephone the potential members on your list to explain the program, solicit their involvement, and if willing, invite their participation.
- Send a letter to the invited members formally appointing them to the advisory board and informing them of the first meeting.

<u>SAMPLE LETTER</u>

Dear (*Advisory Board Member's Name*):

It was good to speak with you today. Thank you for accepting our invitation to join the Advisory Board for the Youthful Offender Program at (*name of the facility*). Your willingness to support our efforts is greatly appreciated, and I look forward to working with you.

Our first Advisory Board Meeting will be on (*date and time*) in my office. I have enclosed directions to the institution. As you come into the main security checkpoint, staff will meet you to escort you to the meeting. I have arranged for a working dinner meeting, and the enclosed agenda will help you prepare for our deliberations. I believe that we will meet for no longer than two hours. Thank you again for your kind offer of help. Should you need to contact me, I may be reached at (*telephone number and e-mail address, if available*).

Sincerely,

The warden also should communicate with the stakeholders who have a vested interest in the institution and the programs offered to inmates. The following are examples of such correspondence:

LETTER TO PROFESSIONALS

This should be sent to such professionals as the chief of police, the superintendent of the local school district, the director of probation, the chief parole officer, and the commissioner of the local social services district, to name but a few.

Dear (*use individual's name*):

I am most pleased to inform you that (*name of institution*) has been selected to house the youthful offender program for the Department of Corrections. C hile we are most eager to meet our new assignment, you know that placing youthful offenders in adult systems provides different challenges for our corrections systems. I want to share with you several of the actions that we have taken for us to continue to meet our mandates.

The youthful offender program is based on correctional best practices and well-researched interventions. Our program model acknowledges that these young offenders, while having committed serious crimes, are still in an active growth period, and so much of what we do is based on sound adolescent development theory. Additionally, we insure that we meet the requirements of statutes, regulations, and agency policies.

The program is highly structured and demands that the youthful offenders be active participants with the staff in the program. The youthful offender program is designed to last (*fill in duration*). At its conclusion, the youthful offenders either will be paroled or moved into the general inmate population. The department has decided to place the youthful offenders at (*insert name of institution(s)*), which is located in your service district.

To best meet the developmental needs of the youthful offenders, we shall offer a variety of programs and services. Some of these are mandated by law, others by regulation, and still others by our position that these youthful offenders will be returning to their communities, and we want them to be prepared to be constructive citizens. The program components include and are not limited to: (*Each department will have to fill in its own program components but should include as examples: education, vocational training, Aggression Replacement Training, recreation, and counseling, to name but a few*).

Because we are committed to the mission and goals of the youthful offender program, we have trained our staff in the following specific areas:

- adolescent development
- cognitive-behavioral approaches to change youthful offender behavior
- behavior management

- security issues
- special needs

Sincerely,

<u>LETTER TO CITIZENS</u>

Dear (*personal salutation to members of the community within a five-mile radius of the institution*):

As a member of the community and one who we consider to be a neighbor, I want to inform you about a new program that is expected to begin within the next thirty days. As you may know, a new law provides for youthful offenders, that is, young people under the criminal age of responsibility, to be placed in adult prisons. As such, our institution has been recommended to house this special group of offenders.

The youthful offender program is based on correctional best practices and well-researched interventions. Our program model acknowledges that these young offenders, while having committed serious crimes, are still in an active growth period, and so much of what we do is based on sound adolescent development theory. Additionally, we insure that we meet the requirements of statutes, regulations, and agency policies.

The program is highly structured and demands that the youthful offenders be active participants with the staff in the program. The youthful offender program is designed to last (*fill in duration*). At its conclusion, the youthful offenders either will be paroled or moved into the general inmate population. As with our other programs, community safety is our foremost objective. The inclusion of this new offender group will not cause any additional risk to our community, our staff, or our current inmate population.

One reason that we are certain of our program direction is that we have designed the youthful offender program to meet the developmental needs of the youthful offenders. We shall offer a variety of programs and services. Some of these are mandated by law, others by regulation, and still others by our position that these youthful offenders will be returning to their communities, and we want them to be prepared to be constructive citizens. The program components include but are not limited to: (*Each department will have to fill in its own program components but should include as examples: education, vocational training, Aggression Replacement Training, recreation, and counseling, to name but a few*).

Because we are committed to the mission and goals of the youthful offender program, we have trained our staff in the following specific areas:

- adolescent development
- cognitive-behavioral approaches to change youthful offender behavior

- behavior management
- security issues
- special needs

Sincerely,

I am the administrator responsible for the youthful offender program. How do I monitor the day-to-day operations of the program, insuring that both the staff and the programs operate efficiently?

The administrator who is responsible for managing and supervising the youthful offender program must insure that there is accurate reporting, information sharing, and direct observation of programs. A variety of strategies may be used, including the following:

- Conduct daily program visits to observe staff, support program principles, and talk with youths.
- Convene weekly managers' meetings with key staff (security administrator, case managers, education supervisor, maintenance supervisor, medical administrator, cook, and recreation therapist).
- Review staff and unit logs every week.
- Require weekly unit reports.
- Conduct inspections.
- Provide staff training at least quarterly.
- Provide consistent supervision of tasks.

To aid the program administrator, the following checklist may be used to facilitate program monitoring:

Program Checklist

1. A. Have all cells including the walls, floors, ceilings, windows, and fixtures been inspected physically? Yes _ No _
   B. Are they in good working order? Yes _ No _
   C. Do they meet health, safety, and security standards? Yes _ No _
2. Are the open areas within the living area (dayrooms, reading rooms, and lavatories) clean, physically attractive, and in good working order? Yes _ No _
3. Are the corridors leading to and from the living areas physically maintained, clean, and secure? Yes _ No _

4. Have all staff who will be in contact with the youthful offender population successfully completed the basic youthful offender training course? Yes _ No _
5. Is there a published plan, policy, and procedure detailing how staff shortages are to be handled? Yes _ No _ (For example, will there be overtime staff resources budgeted for the youthful offender program, and have institutional "relief staff"' been trained to work in the youthful offender program?)
6. A. Is the food service operation adequately prepared for the youthful offender population—specifically, are youthful offender menus certified by a licensed dietician? Yes _ No _

   B. Is the schedule written and published detailing when the youthful offenders will eat? Yes _ No _

   C. Have arrangements for evening snacks been made? Yes _ No _
7. Is the staff familiar with the goals and objectives of the program; their roles, responsibilities, and assignments? Yes _ No _
8. Do supervisors know the details of their shift responsibility such as where they are supposed to be and whom they are to supervise? Yes _ No _

   We believe it is important that supervisors understand the goals, objectives, and philosophy of the program so they may model its principles for staff. It will be the responsibility of the line supervisors to assure that the staff adheres to the basic principles of the program.
9. Do line staff know their assignments and feel comfortable with their assignments? Yes _ No _
10. Do staff know their individual post assignments? Yes _ No

    We have written elsewhere (Glick and Goldstein, 1995) that one major responsibility of a supervisor is to create an environment in which staff can grow and develop, professionally and personally. As such, it is sound management practice to assign staff to tasks which they are willing and able to complete. A successful supervisor knows that forcing staff to work in a program in which they are not motivated to participate, or untrained to implement, or unwilling to support, will create greater problems for the program output, their colleagues, and the youthful offenders placed in it.
11. Does staff know their shift schedule and clearly understand when to take breaks, meals, and perform other scheduled activities? Yes _ No _
12. Does staff know when they are responsible to relieve other staff? Yes _ No _

Chart 3.8 is a detailed sample staff schedule that includes the names of staff, their work assignments, and the times they are on breaks, including meals. It is helpful for the information to be published so all staff, not only supervisors, know the whereabouts of their colleagues.

Chart 3.8

YOUTHFUL OFFENDER STAFF SCHEDULE

Weekdays: (example assumes an 8:00 A.M. to 4 P.M. workday)

Name	Assignment	A.M. Break	Meal Break	P.M. Break	Relief
Captain Smith	Shift Supervisor	9:30 A.M.	11:00 A.M.	2:30 P.M.	4:00 P.M.
Sgt. Green	ACH*/Tier 1	10:00 A.M.	11:00 A.M.	1:45 P.M.	4:00 P.M.
Mr. Gold	GED Teacher	9:30 A.M.	12:00 PM	2:00 PM	4:00 P.M.
Coach Jones	Outdoor Rec.	10:15 A.M.	11:30 A.M.	2:15 P.M.	4:00 P.M.
Ms. White	Program Supervisor	9:45 A.M.	11:30 A.M.	2:00 P.M.	4:00 P.M.
Ms. Rose	Counselor	10:00 A.M.	1:00 P.M.	3:00 P.M.	4:00 P.M.

****Abbreviation for A-Cellhouse***

13. Are there performance outcomes for all program components? Yes _ No _
    Program performance outcomes must be written, observable, measurable, and constantly reinforced by the program director and other staff.
14. Are there procedures and policies (written and practiced) that deal with those offenders who act out in the program? Yes _ No _
15. Is there a detailed daily operational schedule for the youthful offender program? Yes _ No _
    A. Is the daily schedule reviewed? Yes _ No _ By whom?
    (Name) ______________________________ (Title) ______________________________
    B. Have any deficiencies in the schedule been identified, published, and remedied? Yes _ No _

We suggest that the program director conduct several pilot trials of the schedule at various times of the day, to ensure that it is operationally sound. The watchwords are be prepared! That is, always build in contingencies for the unexpected, such as staff not coming to work, accidents on the job, untoward incidents. Since the daily schedule is the basis for the operation of the program, it must be realistic, and it must work. A five-minute delay in one part of the schedule can disrupt the entire schedule for an entire day. We have observed that a delay in movement and/or activities may disrupt staff and youthful offenders in their routine, and many times may affect morale and offender behavior.

16. Is there a mechanism in place to brief the program director about the status of offenders who either are regressing or are failing to progress in their individualized program? Yes _ No _

I am a correctional officer assigned to manage a group of youthful offenders in a special program. What should I do when a youth begins to act out, or starts being disruptive? Is my only choice to restrain, contain, and transfer that youth to administrative segregation?

It is assumed that direct care staff, whether they are correctional officers, teachers, recreation aides, or others who are responsible for the care and supervision of this population, will receive special training in this area. However, there are some tried and tested techniques that help to manage adolescent disruptive behavior. Fritz Redl developed a series of interventions to deal with disruptive adolescent behavior. We suggest that direct line staff receive training in these strategies and practice developing their own style in using these techniques. We will describe these interventions in brief.

Planned Ignoring. This is a skill used by an adult to size up the surface behavior of a youth. Ignore the behavior and limit adult interference only to those behaviors that would not stop on their own, or would create a security violation.

Signal Interference. This is a clear gesture of disapproval (for example, waving a finger or making a nonverbal communication). This technique is contraindicated when there is a disturbance in the relationships between the adult and youth; or where the behavior requires more than a simple nonverbal gesture.

Proximity and Touch Control. Increasing the physical proximity between the adult and the youth alleviates inappropriate behavior (hyperactivity, anxiety, and restlessness). Examples include: moving towards or close to the young person; direct physical contact (such as putting a hand on his or her shoulder); patting the young person on the shoulder with such verbal friendly challenges as "come on," "take it easy," "snap out of it."

Involvement in Interest Relationship. This is the deliberate involvement of an adult in the youth's activity. Showing interest by asking questions such as "what are you doing?" or providing information about a particular situation, involves the adult and demonstrates interest in what the young person is doing.

Hypodermic Affection. This may include sudden, unexpected, or an additional quantity of affection. Hypodermic affection does not dissolve or cure tendencies toward temper tantrums or negative behavior nor does it assuage all instances of aggression.

Tension-decontamination through Humor. This is a well-planned and timed attempt at "kidding the young person out of the situation." This works because we demonstrate the invulnerability of the adult (self-confident and secure). It is face-saving for the youth. It reduces feelings of guilt or pressure to "act tough." The young person is perceived as having a sense of humor by peers. *Caution: There is a difference between humor and ironic sarcasm or cynicism (which increases aggression).*

Hurdle Help. This is adult support and help which allows the young person to get over the situation in which he or she is stuck.

Interpretation as Interference. This is an attempt to help the young person understand the meaning of a situation that he or she has misinterpreted.

Regrouping. This is a change in the group's social/psychological constellation. Types of regrouping include total regrouping (for example, transfer to administrative segregation); compositional regrouping (for example, changing a youthful offender's "cell block or cell); distributional regrouping (for example, changing assignments or projects).

Restructuring. This is abandoning the activity or situation that is causing the acting-out behavior (for example, having offenders exercise when they look drowsy).

Direct Appeal. This includes a petition or request by the adult to the young person to cease the behavior. ("Please, John, not now, I am really tired".)

Frequently used appeals (examples for each are in parentheses):

- **Appeal to Personal Relationship** ("You and I have worked too hard on this problem for you to behave this way, at this time.")
- **Physical Reality Implication** ("C'mon John, he is half your size, and you know you can beat his hide, so why bother.")
- **Undesirable Consequences Inherent in the Act** ("If you continue to disregard my warnings, I will have no alternative but to remove you from the group, and I don't want to do that, and you don't need that to happen now either.")
- **Outside Role Sensitivities** ("I am not a nurse, and cannot do that kind of work, so you need to wait until medical call in about an hour.")
- **Superego Demand and Value Sensitivity** ("My conscience just won't allow me to let you hit him, now or later, so please stop.")
- **Group Code Values** ("Our group rules state that no one may hurt themselves or others. Therefore, I cannot allow you to continue to behave in this way.")

- **Appraisal of Community Consequences** ("If you continue to take things that don't belong to you, the group may decide to have you moved to another unit. Since you have stated you don't want to move to another cell block, doesn't it seem reasonable that you rethink what you are doing and stop it?")
- **Awareness of Peer Group Reaction** ("You know what the group stated last week when you behaved irresponsibly. This is no different, and so I would hope you will reconsider what you are doing and stop these actions immediately.")
- **Hierarchical Limitation Awareness** ("You know there is a chain of command here, and I have no authority to allow you to do that. If you wait until the warden returns, I will ask him/her about your request.")
- **Personal Considerations** ("You have but two months left before discharge. You know better.")
- **Pride in Personal Improvement** ("John, you have done so well over the last three months, you can make it through this situation if you just stop and think about how well you have done thus far.")

Limitation of Space and Tools. This includes a limit on space and tools through avoidance, that is, locking the material away, subjecting its use to conditions and rules, or removing the material from the young person.

Antiseptic Bouncing. Removing the young person from the situation because of physical danger; group psychodynamics; uncheckable contagion effects; need to save face; or limit setting for others. Antiseptic bouncing is not throwing the young person out with anger or triumph.

Physical Restraint. This is the physical containment of a young person who is "out of control." This should be used as a "last-resort" intervention, since it makes the adult powerless.

Staff Training

I am responsible for staff training for the department and have been assigned to support and facilitate training for the staff of a recently implemented youthful offender program. Help!

Staff training is a critical area that must be managed well for a youthful offender program to be implemented successfully. Staff assigned to a youthful offender program, either mandated or self-selected, are usually competent when dealing with adult offenders. However, youthful offenders, by virtue of their developmental adolescent needs, require staff who are aware of adolescent development, but also have other skill areas such as behavior management; knowledge of nutrition as it impacts youth behavior; awareness of suicide prevention; clarity in staff roles and boundaries; and communications and report writing, to name but a few. The individual responsible for staff development should accomplish at least the following:

- Perform a staff survey and training needs assessment.
- Determine policy direction for the type of training, its duration, and the resources.
- Develop a training plan that includes training curricula for the youthful offender program staff and lists specifics as to when training will occur; how it will be delivered; by whom; how long it will take to complete the initiative; and some recommendation of budget costs.

TRAINING ADMINISTRATOR'S CHECKLIST OF QUESTIONS

1. What are the core courses of the youthful offender curriculum?

   _ Adolescent development (We recommend that this be mandatory). Adolescent development should be the cornerstone course of the training curriculum. Staff must have a thorough understanding of how adolescents develop and how that development influences their everyday behavior.

   Other core courses:

   _ Shifting paradigms.

   _ Suicide recognition and prevention. Adolescents constantly make threats of suicide, have a suicidal ideation, and sometimes display suicidal gestures. The staff must be instructed to observe youthful offenders constantly and report any of the signals that may be dangerous.

   _ Staff boundaries. Staff must learn how to interact with adolescents to facilitate their growth and development. Staff need to be perceived as caring adults, committed to youth development and individual growth. However, they must not behave as the youthful offenders' "friend," "buddy," or in other intimate relationships.

   _ Interpersonal communications. These are the messages we give to adolescents, based on their developmental stage. This includes: what we communicate, how we communicate it, the tone of our voice, and our body language. All of these factors must be orchestrated carefully if we are to have an impact on the developmental growth of this population.

   _ Program overview. This is a summary of all the programs offered to youthful offenders in the youthful offender program, the rationale for why these programs are offered, and information on how staff can support the outcomes of each in their daily work.

2. What is the duration of the training?

   We recommend that training not be less than forty hours. It is important that there be adequate time for the staff to learn concepts, apply their learning in practical class activities, and then understand how this information is used and applied in their daily work with the youthful offender.

3. Who will deliver the training?
   Identifying personnel to conduct the training will take some effort and should be included in the agency's training plan for this program. It is crucial that those trainers delivering the training be well-versed in adolescent development, program delivery, security, and adult prison operations. The American Correctional Association offers training through one of its grant programs and the National Institute of Corrections offers a Youthful Offenders Training for Trainers' Course through technical assistance grants.

4. Who will receive the training?
   It is important for the training staff to identify any and all staff who will have any interaction with the youthful offender population. Very often, the following important groups are overlooked for youthful offender training. However, they play a vital role in the total management structure of the system, and, as such, should be included:

   _ Dietary staff
   _ Industry staff
   _ Library staff, including legal library staff
   _ Maintenance staff
   _ Volunteers and the volunteer coordinator
   _ Facility warden
   _ Deputy wardens for programs and security
   _ School counselors
   _ Central office personnel
   _ Classification staff
   _ Medical staff
   _ Programs staff
   _ Food service staff
   _ Financial staff

5. Where will the training be delivered?
   If possible, the training should be conducted at the facility where the program will be housed. This will give the participants an opportunity to view the different areas where the program's activities will take place. However, there is risk in having the training on-site, since routine tasks of staff or legitimate emergency situations may distract them. Yet, by having this firsthand experience, the participants will be able to:

Coordinate the program activities with the physical space requirements
Become familiar with the physical security of the:
_ Living area
_ Recreation area (s)
_ Educational area (s)
_ Dining area
_ Visiting area
_ Religious area

6. What is the timetable for the training ?
The basic youthful offender training should be concluded no sooner than two weeks before the start-up of the program. If the initial staff is trained too far in advance of the program, staff may not remember all of what they are taught during training, and staff who have received the initial training may be transferred and/or promoted to positions that would exclude them from participating in the program. There should be at least two additional basic training courses offered within the first eight-or-nine months of the program start-up. This would cushion whatever staff turnover occurs and allow for a cadre of competent staff to work with the youthful offenders. Finally, the training plan should include the dates when additional basic youthful offender training is scheduled and provide a model for an annual training curriculum for existing youthful offender program staff.

Program Information and Dissemination

Part of the youthful offender program's success is contingent on how well information is developed and disseminated. It is all staff's responsibility to know about the program, its mission, goals, and objectives. It is also staff's responsibility to support the program philosophy and direction. We have seen a direct and significant relationship between the level of staff involvement, and the motivation staff has toward serving this difficult population. It is the responsibility of the warden and the youthful offender program director to translate the agency's vision, mission, goals, and objectives into written material.

While the agency's public information office may take the lead to publish the final public documents, the program experts must provide a substantive foundation for those materials. It is good to begin with a sound program description for the youthful offender program. The document should include at the very least:

– A statement of philosophy about the program, how and why it was developed, and the basis on which it operates.
_ A statement of the mission, goals, and objectives of the program.

- The nature of staff who work within the program, including the standards and expectations for their actions and interactions with each other and the youthful offenders (for example, staff involvement, initiative, understanding of self, understanding of others, openness to communication, listening ability, ability to communicate, use of feedback, and participation in the decision-making processes).
- A description of the program components: education; vocational training; occupational choice exploration; counseling; cognitive behavior program interventions; and recreation.
- Safety and security procedures such as: youth movement; use of language (for example, tone of voice, no profanity); wake-up routine; quiet time (use of leisure); snacks; infirmary and sick call, to name but a few.)

Once these concepts have been detailed, the public information office and staff can begin their work.

Role of the Public Information Officer

I am the public information officer for the department and charged with developing materials for the youthful offender program. What information do I need to include and in what format?

The materials that are developed should have fundamental information that may be tailored to specific audiences. Toward that end, the public information officer needs to insure that the following information is developed and that the following questions are answered:

- Why has the department decided to establish a youthful offender program?
- What is the program's mission statement?
- What are the program's goals and objectives?
- What is the theoretical basis on which the program has been developed and designed?
- What is the duration of the program?
- How many youthful offenders are now in the program? How many are expected to be in the program?
- What staff comprises the program? What are their roles and functions? What type of training, experience, and qualifications do they have?
- Who is the person responsible for administering the program?
- Where is the program located?
- What are the department's standards for the program's safety and security? What policies and procedures have been promulgated to insure community safety and institutional safety for staff and offenders?

_ What steps will the department take to insure the community's involvement with the program? This includes an institutional advisory board, a mentoring program, a public service program, and use of volunteers.

Once the information has been developed, packets of material should be prepared to be included with correspondence that may be sent from the department or the institution housing the program. Additionally, stakeholders also will need to receive targeted information critical to their own area of interest. As such, packets should be included for the following groups:

- Executives of jurisdictions (counties, cities, towns, and villages)
- The legislature (both state and municipal)
- The judiciary (adult and family courts)
- The professional community (probation, parole, social services, and education—local education agencies, community colleges, and technical training schools)
- The public community (neighbors, visitors, and families)

Finally, the public information officer needs to insure that the information is updated regularly with data, statistics, and new program initiatives. This information may be distributed within the department and to the general community in quarterly newsletters and information bulletins. A routine communication will go a long way to insure public support for the program.

Program Monitoring and Accountability

There are many good programs available to corrections professionals, programs that work, programs that have been evaluated and have been shown to be effective. Yet, these programs, when replicated in other places, even within the same systems in which they were developed, fail miserably. Very often, correctional systems start and stop programs, concluding that they do not work, or they are not the right matches for their particular offender population. Unfortunately, many programs that are well designed and implemented successfully are prematurely stopped because of impulsive managers who did not take the time to monitor what was happening with the program, nor hold the staff accountable for their tasks and responsibilities in the program.

Program monitoring—that is, the methodical inspection and oversight of a particular program intervention—is a specific, deliberate supervisory activity. It is not difficult to accomplish, nor does it require a complicated procedure. It does take time, a bit of ingenuity, and the perseverance to observe what is happening on a consistent and regular basis. The accountability factors involved in this process include well-established administrative techniques such as data collection; objective observations; summaries and conclusions relevant to the activities observed; and immediate, specific, fair, and considerate feedback to staff.

The information collected should answer at least two basic questions. First, was the program implemented as designed? Second, did the program achieve the desired results? These two questions should dictate the information gathered, whether it is by staff interview, offender interview, checklist, staff survey, or manager's reports. When designing a monitoring system, one should consider the following:

- What do we want for our youthful offenders, their families, and communities?
- How will we know if the program we have designed and implemented is working as well as possible?
- How will we know if we have achieved the goals and objectives of the program?
- Does our monitoring system establish a standard for the performance of staff and offenders?
- Can we monitor staff performance against objective standards?
- Is there a way to measure the level of compliance with the established standards?
- Can we identify the program dimensions and components and incorporate these in our monitoring system, whether it be through an observational checklist or a manager's narrative?

I am the program director responsible for monitoring the youthful offender program and insuring its accountability as developed, designed, and implemented by the department. What information should I collect?

<u>PROGRAM MONITORING WEEKLY CHECKLIST</u>

1. Number of youthful offenders in each stage (phase, level, or however the program is structured):

   Stage One: ________

   Stage Two: ________

   Stage Three: ________

   Stage Four: ________

2. Number of youthful offenders in disciplinary segregation: _______.

   Name(s) of youthful offenders and time remaining in disciplinary segregation:

Name:___________ Time Served: _____________ Time Remaining:_____________

Name:___________ Time Served: _____________ Time Remaining:_____________

Name:___________ Time Served: _____________ Time Remaining:_____________

3. Number of youthful offenders in administrative segregation: ________.
Name(s) of youthful offenders and time remaining in administrative segregation:
Name:____________ Time Served: ______________ Time Remaining:____________
Name:____________ Time Served: ______________ Time Remaining:____________
Name:____________ Time Served: ______________ Time Remaining:____________

4. A. Are the menus posted in offender living areas? _Yes _ No
B. Do staff and youthful offenders in the program know the meal schedule? _Yes __No
C. Is the schedule followed? _ Yes _ No

Using military times, here is one schedule.

Phase One	**1130**	**Main Dining Area**
Phase Two	**1145**	**Main Dining Area**
Phase Three	**1200**	**"A" Cellhouse**

Group Counseling

5. A. Is the group counseling schedule posted? _ Yes _ No
B. Do staff and youthful offenders know what the group counseling schedule is? _ Yes _ No
C. Is the group counseling schedule followed? _ Yes _ No

Here is a sample schedule.

Name	**Time**	**Location**	**Staff Person**
Substance Abuse	**18:30 hrs**	**Dayroom B Cell House,**	**Ms. Smith**

Enter names of group participants here:

Staff Schedules

6. A. Number of staff who are on duty? ________
B. Names of staff on duty:

7. Names of staff who have days off, reasons for their time off (training, vacation, sick leave, administrative leave, other), and their days off.

Names:	Reason:	Dates:	Training:

8. Staff Post Assignments. The following charts should be compiled.

Security Supervisors' Name and Shift

Name: Lt.	Midnight
Name: Lt.	Day
Name: Lt.	Evening
Name: Lt.	Relief

Here is a sample list of staff assignments.

SECURITY STAFFING ASSIGNMENTS BY NAME AND POSTS

Schedules such as the following should be completed.

Assignment	Name	Shift
"A" Cellhouse	Sgt.	Day
"A" Cellhouse	CO	Day
"A" Cellhouse	Utility Officer	Day
"A" Cellhouse	Utility Officer CO	Day
"A" Cellhouse	Sgt.	Evening
"A" Cellhouse	CO	Evening
"A" Cellhouse	Sgt.	Midnight
"A" Cellhouse	CO	Midnight
"B" Cellhouse	Sgt.	Day
"B" Cellhouse	CO	Day
"B" Cellhouse	Sgt.	Evening
"B" Cellhouse	CO	Evening
"B" Cellhouse	CO	Evening
"B" Cellhouse	Sgt.	Midnight
"B" Cellhouse	CO	Midnight

PROGRAM SUPERVISOR'S NAME, LOCATION, AND SHIFT

Name: Dr.	Administration Bldg	Day
Name: Ms. MSW	"A" Cellhouse	Day
Name: Mr. MSW	"B" Cellhouse	Day
Name: Counselor	"A" Cellhouse	Evening
Name: Counselor	"B" Cellhouse	Evening

RECREATION SCHEDULE BY PHASE, TIME, RECREATION SPECIALIST, AND AREA

Phase One	0730	Coach (Name)	Main Recreation Yard
Phase Two	1230	Coach (Name)	"A" Cellhouse Recreation Yard
Phase Three	1315	Coach (Name)	"B" Cellhouse Recreation Yard

PROGRAM SCHEDULES

10. Is the education schedule posted and followed? _ Yes _ No

(A.M. Education	0800) - 1015	(A.M. Break)	1030-1200
(P.M. Education	1300) - 1415	(P.M. Break)	1430-1700

11. Is the institutional work schedule posted and followed? _ Yes _ No

(A.M. Work)	0700 - 0915	(A.M. Break)	0930 - 1130
(P.M. Work)	1230 - 1400	(P.M. Break)	1415 - 1645

RECREATION WEEKLY SCHEDULE

DAY /TIME	ACTIVITY/PHASE	LOCATION	STAFF PERSON
Sunday 0930-1030	Volleyball - Phase One	Main Recreation Yard	Coach (Name)
Sunday 1400-1500	Volleyball - Phase Two	Main Recreation Yard	Coach (Name)
Sunday 1830-1930	Volleyball - Phase Three	Main Recreation Yard	Coach (Name)
Monday 0700-0730	Physical Fitness- Phase One	Cellhouse "A" Rec. Yard	Coach (Name)
Monday 0730-0800	Physical Fitness- Phase Two	Cellhouse "A" Rec. Yard	Coach (Name)

Complete this section for each of the days of the week in the same way.

Submitted by:______________________________ Date:________________________

PROGRAMS SCHEDULE FOR THE WEEK OF ____________

DAY /TIME	PROGRAM/PHASE	LOCATION	STAFF PERSON
Sunday/0800	Catholic Services	Main Chapel	Fr. (Name)
Sunday/0900	Protestant Services	Main Chapel	Rev. (Name)
Sunday/1400-1500	Visiting	"Y" Visiting Area	Sgt. (Name)
Sunday/1830-1930	Movie; Reward	Living Area	Housing Supervisor
Monday/1330-1430	Anger Management-Phase 1	"A" CH Multi-Purpose Rm.	Dr. (Name)
Monday/1445-1545	Anger Management-Phase 1	"B" CH Multi-Purpose Rm.	Dr. (Name)
Monday/1600-1700	Individual Counseling-Phase 2	"B" CH Multi-Purpose Rm.	Dr. (Name)
Monday/1800-1900	Group Counseling	"A"CH Multi-Purpose Rm.	Dr. (Name)
Monday/1900-2000	Group Counseling	"B"CH Multi-Purpose Rm.	Dr. (Name)

Complete this section in detail as illustrated above for each of the days of the week.

Submitted by:______________________________ Date:______________

PROGRAM EVALUATION AND RESEARCH

It is unfortunate that many correctional systems resist evaluating their programs and conducting research on their efforts to obtain program outcomes and results. There are many reasons why this condition exists. Perhaps it is the mystique that program evaluators have led us to believe exists in conducting research. Or, maybe it is the administrators of programs who must plan to include a bona fide program evaluation and research design when implementing programs, who do not consider it important. It could be due to our own opinion that research activities are "academic" and have no place in the operations of corrections systems.

Whatever the reason, the lack of a planned, well-integrated program evaluation as part of the program design and implementation continues to be a flaw in the system. Without efficacy and outcome results, the best of programs are vulnerable to attacks from budget analysts who believe money ought to be spent on operations, not programs; security proponents who do not care whether programs exist at all in correctional systems; and staff who are unsure if their efforts make any difference at all.

We strongly urge that program evaluation and research be an integral part of the program development, design, and implementation plan from its inception. All too often, we invite researchers to evaluate programs only after they have been operational for a while. Indeed, program administrators responsible for design and development should insure that program evaluators/researchers are at the planning table as the project begins, not after the program is implemented. In that way, these individuals will be able to understand what the agency wants to accomplish, understand the nature of the program, and advise the program developers on how to integrate research and program evaluation methods into daily routines, without being disruptive to either program, staff, or youthful offenders.

Research designs and program evaluations need not be complex or so complicated that corrections staff cannot help in their development and implementation. In fact, we believe that if staff cannot understand why they use a particular research protocol or evaluation instrument, it ought not to be considered. Research should be practical. Program evaluation should be sensible. And staff should value the utility of both to their own jobs, making their work environment easier, and more rewarding and satisfying. Toward these ends, we suggest youthful offender program administrators consider the following:

- Invite researchers and program evaluators to the initial program design and development meeting and consider them an integral part of the team.
- Insure that evaluation and research designs are simple.
- Have all research instruments reviewed by the youthful offender program staff to insure the instruments are practical and useful to program operations.
- Refrain from "mystifying" research, and force researchers to explain concepts in terms that all can understand.
- Realize that researchers and program evaluators work for the program staff. It is their responsibility to design research to meet program needs.
- Compromise and take initiative to stretch the program paradigm to accommodate program evaluation. Do not be quick to dismiss evaluation processes as incompatible with program operations.
- Invite direct line staff to recommend changes in evaluation designs or research based on their own experience and training, and incorporate their comments wherever and whenever possible.
- Empower program staff to consider the merits of program evaluation by providing them with information about how the results will be used to modify program operations, justify budgets, influence policy makers, and empower them as practitioners.

We have had good success in developing and implementing research and program evaluations using these suggestions. In addition, many of these principles are applicable to most program development components. Toward that end, correctional administrators should not abdicate their responsibilities and influence in this area.

I am an administrator responsible for the youthful offender program and have been asked to include appropriate research and program evaluation components. My agency has a small research unit. What are my next steps?

1. Consult with the agency's research unit to determine if they are able to join the program development and design group.
2. Provide the research unit with a copy of the program description, highlighting the program's mission, goals, and objectives.
3. Instruct the assigned research staff to provide the group with simple and concrete information on how research and program evaluation may be included in their program design.
4. Be prepared to communicate with the program staff about the research efforts through staff meetings, individual staff conversations, informal chats (lunchroom, bathroom, coffee breaks), formal memoranda, and newsletters.
5. Listen to the researcher's requirements and bottom lines for proper evaluations and integrate those with program operations' needs by allowing staff to design the details with the research staff.
6. Administratively mediate and/or arbitrate differences of opinions or disputes between research/program evaluation and program needs—objectively, fairly and impartially, without compromising the goals of each.
7. As the administrator, maintain the agency vision as the benchmark of your efforts and never, ever take such positions as "impossible," "it can't be done," "we have always done it that way," or other program-paralyzing positions. Always demand a compromise toward an operational solution.

I am an administrator responsible for the youthful offender program and have been asked to include appropriate research and program evaluation components. However, my agency either has no research capability or the research unit cannot include this project within its existing workload. What are my next steps?

1. Inform the chief executive officer of the situation and seek approval to find research capability outside the agency.

2. Search for universities close to the institution and determine if any are able to provide support for your initiative, either voluntarily or for fees. *Note:* Very often university departments of criminal justice, social work, and counseling, as examples, have graduate students who need research projects to complete degree requirements. Also, some universities already have established working relationships with correctional systems and may be able to accommodate such requests.
3. Provide information verbally and in writing to the university center, followed by a meeting to discuss mutual interests and needs.
4. Consummate a written agreement with the university center (as a voluntary, no-fee project; or a contract) specifically outlining the scope of the project, the duration, the agency's and university's responsibilities, outcomes, and the next steps.

AGREEMENT BETWEEN A CORRECTIONAL SYSTEM AND A UNIVERSITY CENTER

This is to formalize the agreement between (name of correctional system) and (name of university center or department) to provide research and program evaluation technical assistance for the youthful offender program planned for (name specific location, either institution or community-based system).

The length of this agreement is for (specify exact time, not less than one year), during which time the university will provide (number and level of graduate students) to participate in the program design, the program evaluation, and the research efforts.

The university will provide the following:

(List here the specific services provided. These may include but not be limited to such activities as research methods, data collection, data entry and analysis, research progress reports, research final report, and student supervision.)

The agency will provide the following:
(List here the specific services provided. These may include but should not be limited to such things as: office spaces, support services—photocopying, secretarial help, supplies and materials—meals while in the institution, program supervision.)

The following products will be delivered as a result of this project:
(List the specific deliverables for both systems.)

Get authorized signatures of both the correctional system and the university.

Inform staff of the research and program evaluation project and the mutually agreed on products. Begin the research project and monitor its progress.

Summary

We have provided in this chapter grass roots, nuts and bolts, how to's and what if's, a series of interventions for correctional systems to consider when developing and designing a youthful offender program. We have not provided answers for all contingencies; however, we have provided fundamental strategies to deal with the operations of the design, development, and implementation for a youthful offender program. We hope that the foundation we have provided, and the directions we suggest, allow the correctional staff who are responsible for the youthful offender program to build on these principles so that their youthful offender program is successful and meets their agency's vision and expectations.

Chapter 5

Where Do We Go From Here?

We started this journey not of our own choosing. Policy makers, reacting to the cries of citizens for community safety and accountability for youth who commit violent crimes, have directed that children, some as young as ten years of age, be incarcerated in adult prisons. For at least thirty-seven jurisdictions throughout the United States, there is no more debate as to whether it is prudent and in the best interest of public policy to place young people under the age of criminal responsibility, according to their own local law, in adult prisons. There are more than 15,000 young people under their local legal age of majority serving adult sentences in adult correctional systems. While we have stated that the chapter is still being written about the outcome of this policy direction, we must take action now to safeguard the welfare of the offenders in our charge.

We do not endorse placing youth in adult prisons as a policy, nor do we believe that in the long run, such action will deter youth violence, youth crime, or recidivism. The strategy we support to prevent young people from committing crimes is to provide prevention programs, early and in sufficient types and quantities, to mitigate against the criminogenic conditions that lead to criminal behavior in the first instance.

This is not a liberal or a conservative position, nor is it partisan politics. It is simply based on what is good human development theory, and our firm belief that the application of adolescent development principles will better insure a safe community and less juvenile and youth crime. We do not support allowing young criminals to escape accountability for their behaviors; however, we do subscribe to appropriate placement and adequate services to meet the targeted needs of the youth population. To do less is irresponsible and will yield a more hardened antisocial person. We maintain that such an individual will be a hybrid of the adult offender that currently exists, modified by their own experience with the street. Unfortunately, because of our policy of incarcerating young persons in adult systems, youthful offenders will have matured in an adult correctional environment during a period of their human growth that is more intense and active than any other, except for infancy and neonatal development. Incarcerating youthful offenders in adult prisons is a condition that is flawed, especially when we think that harsher punishments will deter criminal behavior and create safer communities.

Yet, we have these young offenders in our systems. That is why we believe it is imperative that individuals understand the issues as we first detailed in *No Time to Play* (Glick and Sturgeon, 1998). It is our goal with this monograph to provide the strategic approaches and operational tactics to implement effective and efficient programs for youthful offenders. We have provided the correctional practitioner with models to better manage young offenders in adult corrections systems. We have provided examples to illustrate sound principles of practice and techniques that work. These are based on our own firsthand experience of working with young offenders for more than thirty years. We have sought others' experiences by conducting hundreds of interviews with correctional staff who work well with this population. We have visited institutions across the United States to seek out the best practices that work with young offenders in both the juvenile and adult systems (*see Glick and Rhine, Journal of Correctional Best Practices: Juveniles in Adult Correctional Systems*).

Finally, we have met with young offenders themselves, both those still incarcerated and those who have been released and, at least for the present, they seem to be contributing, constructive citizens within their communities. We are confident that based on these various inputs, our suggestions and techniques are qualitatively relevant. Many of the suggestions we have provided are being evaluated for efficacy in such jurisdictions as South Carolina, Louisiana, Washington, Colorado, Texas, Ohio, Pennsylvania, Nebraska, and Oklahoma, to name but a few. Yet, much work in this area needs to be accomplished.

Back to the Future

To look toward the future, we must visit the past. Indeed, if we do not understand our history, we are destined to repeat it. As such, we must begin with the advent of the first juvenile court, which was established in 1899 in Cook County (Chicago) Illinois. The original intent of that legislation was to establish a court that would attend to the best interests of the child who committed crimes or was dependent and neglected, and apply appropriate youth development practices to each case. That first juvenile court was the benchmark on which other courts were established, to insure that young people were provided the best care available and to prevent them from being institutionalized, either in poorhouses or prisons.

The juvenile court system has served the criminal justice system well during the past hundred years, and has provided social and family services to hundreds of thousands of young people. We have learned from the first public policy redirection that primary and secondary prevention, in other words, interventions focused on keeping young persons out of the bowels of criminal justice systems, met two important objectives. First, such prevention provided opportunities for young people to correct their antisocial behaviors in a supervised and planned, nonincarcerated environment. Second, it provided a less costly alternative to institutionalization. Indeed, for the most part, the juvenile court system has provided alternative interventions for young offenders, which have contributed to lower taxpayer costs for institutionalization and safer neighborhoods.

A second social event in the early twentieth century was the protection of children under the Fair Labor Standards Act. The law stated that children could not work in certain hazardous jobs until they were eighteen years of age. It also limited the number of hours children between the ages of sixteen and eighteen could work while school was in session.

These laws also limited when underage children (between the ages of fourteen and sixteen) could work.

The advent of this social policy direction refocused communities, especially agrarian and manufacturing industries, to begin to value young people as resources in which they needed to invest and who needed to be nurtured, rather than viewing them as chattel or assets. This critically important change fostered the development of education systems, occupational exploration, and career development programs, that emphasized child development and stimulated the beginning of schools of psychology that created a host of new professions and jobs. These included elementary school teachers, counselors, psychologists, early childhood specialists, and pediatricians, to name but a few. The important lesson for the correctional systems and those who set the policies for such systems is that when children are valued and their futures are well planned, society's investment in their most precious resource, their children, leads to economic advantage and an era of less crime, not more.

By the middle of the twentieth century, advances in science and technology led to faster, easier living. The age of modern appliances, television, frozen dinners, ease of transportation, and the combination of high technology with increased expendable income, allowed parents to engage in varied activities. No longer were parents tied to the home. Women entered the work force in greater numbers. There was relative world peace, and children were allowed to explore their environments with greater liberal activities. There were also insidious dangers. Drugs became more popular, and violence was transformed from the battlefields of World War II and the Korean War to the silver screen and some television programs.

One significant social revolution that occurred was the advent of the Beatnik movement. Born in Greenwich Village, New York, these flower children adopted the philosophy of live and let live, peace not war. They created, listened to, and played a new type of music, and introduced the popular use of drugs, such as marijuana, heroin, and cocaine. Beatniks dropped out of the mainstream society, leaving their jobs and hanging out on street corners. They let their hair grow, distributed flowers to anyone they encountered to demonstrate their peaceful intentions, hid their eyes behind sunglasses, and talked of "brotherly love" and "do your thing, as long as you do not hurt someone else in the process." As the decade of the fifties ended, the movement drew less attention and became less popular. However, the Beatnik movement dramatically changed the fiber of American culture influencing how people related to each other and how parents reared their children.

More importantly, the Beatnik movement provided the foundation for other counterculture groups. In fact, the Hippie movement of the 1970s was fundamentally based on and influenced by the Beatnik generation. This included much of the music, the advent of open and liberal sexual activities, the wide use of drugs, liberal attitudes toward social rules, less organized religion, and less structure. Parents allowed children to freely choose what they wanted to do, when they did it, and how. Parents provided less supervision to older children and adolescents. Few limits were placed on what children viewed in movies, listened to at music concerts, and little attention was paid to peer associates, educational achievement, and future planning.

The lax attitude toward social organization, standards of supervision, and deliberate, planned goal setting and achievement allowed a generation of children to develop with less discipline, less value placed on social interactions, and more ability to take another's perspective. This situation was most deleterious because no one at that time considered the impact of our communal actions on future growth, attitude formation, and a rather insidious move toward egocentric, hedonistic values held by our children, who one day would inherit our world. Critical to this condition was a tolerance for less social skill development, lower academic prowess, and greater insensitivity about the common good.

Almost simultaneously, two separate but interdependent social phenomena occurred. These were the introduction of crack cocaine in the heart of our youth population and the easy accessibility and access to handguns. These two conditions combined with a generation that had been desensitized to aggression and violence by television, movies, and newspapers, thus creating ripe conditions for young children and adolescents to commit heinous crimes and perpetrate havoc in their schools and communities.

If we believe the basic tenets of adolescence as we have previously described (Glick and Sturgeon, 1998), then we should have predicted that these combinations of events would lead to where we are. Yet, prophets who warned of these conditions leading to greater violence (Goldstein and Segal, 1983; Apter and Goldstein, 1986) were not heeded, and, indeed, were scorned for the positions they took. The rest is history. By the 1990s, communities were hopelessly incapacitated by their ability to create safe and secure neighborhoods, citizens locked themselves behind closed doors in the perceived safety of their own homes, and young people began to coalesce into groups to either harass others or to protect themselves.

Finally, we would be remiss if we did not also identify gangs as a major contributor to youth crime and violence. These social groups have been around for a long time. Gangs are not a new phenomenon, nor are gangs more violent or more vicious than their earlier counterparts. In the twentieth century alone, there have been at least three waves of gang activities within the United States.

Beginning with the turn of the century when the first Eastern Europeans emigrated to the United States, and there was an increase in ethnic groups, gangs took on the characteristics of old country authority, protector, and enforcer. In New York City, for example, the

Delancy Street Boys fought furiously with their ethnic Slavic enemies on Canal Street, not five blocks away. We all know about the gang warfare in Chicago during the twenties in which the federal government (remember Eliot Ness) attempted to suppress the gangland activities of Al Capone, who reigned as king.

By the time the fifties arrived, the social fiber, as we have previously discussed, had taken root. As such, gangs became more sophisticated and selected appointed times and rituals for their activities. *West Side Story*, the famous musical, depicts much of the gang influence of the time. Finally, economic conditions that prevailed in the 1980s also had an impact on gang evolution. During this time, gangs such as the Bloods, the Crips, the Latin Kings, and the Netas became popular.

Today, gangs are major corporations, using sophisticated technology such as computers, cell phones, and the Internet to conduct their business and to create a society in which their members thrive. It is the business of power, profit, and control (Glick and Sturgeon, 1998) that are the fundamental operating principles for the modern gang.

Current Realities

We learn in elementary physics classes that given the opportunity, nature always will fill a vacuum. That principle also applies to social policy. In the absence of policy, society will attempt to fill that void with some strategy or tactical operation to insure a balance or equilibrium for social order. In the absence of a national youth policy, jurisdictions at all governmental levels may legislate to insure safe communities, and satisfy constituent opinion. Indeed, that has been the case in twenty-eight states in which legislation has been passed to treat youthful offenders as adults, adjudicating and sentencing them to adult institutions based on the crimes they commit.

In addition, we know from Newton's laws of physics that for every action, there is an equal and opposite reaction. That has been the case in the promulgation of statutes and court procedures for youthful offenders. Based on the *FBI* crime statistics reports throughout the early 1990s, as well as citizens' intolerance for unsafe communities and youth violence in their neighborhoods, many jurisdictions passed youthful offender laws, placing young people in adult systems. These actions were an "equal and opposite reaction" to youth crime based on political responses to perceived threats by the youth population. It is true that youth violent crime had increased in the latter part of the 1980s and the first four years of the 1990s. However, the assertion by political stakeholders and community citizens that the juvenile court system was inept and the juvenile justice system was unable to deal with this new breed of juvenile violent offender was a backlash to a social condition without any national policy direction.

Let us review what the current situation and positions are. We know:

- Based on current experience, youth are incarcerated, proportionately, for longer periods of time than their adult counterparts for similar offenses.
- The current adult systems are competent to manage adult prisoners but need training and reorientation to manage youth in adult systems.
- Most adult corrections systems are not designed for, nor do they provide, adequate basic services to meet youths' social, emotional, cognitive, and physical needs, growth, and development.
- Only one-half of 1 percent of the adolescent population commit violent crimes, and the majority of the adolescent population are honorable, law-abiding, contributing citizens of society.
- Communities have not become safer as a result of incarcerating youths in adult correctional systems for longer periods of time.
- Communities that have made a concerted effort to reestablish social order and authority controlled by its citizens experience less criminal activity and greater citizen involvement in keeping neighborhoods safe and free from crime.
- Law enforcement that works in concert with local communities is successful in reducing neighborhood criminal activity and increasing perceived community safety.
- The criminal justice system has developed ways to intervene in criminal behavior and to reduce recidivism.
- Research has demonstrated that certain factors correlate more highly with criminal behavior than others.
- Cognitive behavior programs have been demonstrated to be effective interventions for offenders, targeting specific deficit areas such as cognitive skills, moral reasoning, and anger control.
- There is little or no evidence that harsher punishment effectively reduces criminal behavior among youthful offenders nor does incarceration deter future criminal behavior among the youth population.
- Some adult correctional systems have developed different paradigms and are exploring alternative interventions to deal with youthful offenders placed in their systems (*see Glick and Rhine, Journal of Correctional Best Practices: Juveniles in Adult Correctional Systems*, 2001).

Our current reality, however, does not take into consideration many of the principles we have described thus far in this monograph. Many of our colleagues continue to manage and implement their systems as if these youthful offenders were just a part of their existing population. That approach is simply flawed and leads to many of the issues we already have addressed. More important to our existing paradigm paralysis (Barker, 1992) is what we fail to address and identify as a result of our current methods and vision.

We have failed to understand that these youthful offenders are developing through a vitally active growth period. Without planned, deliberate programs, they will evolve into a more vicious, hybrid criminal type for which we have no inoculation. We have not thought about the havoc these matured criminals, who have grown up in our prisons, may reap on our communities on their release. Nor have we yet understood that it will take more of our scarce resources to keep this population in our institutions for potentially longer periods of time. This is occurring during a time when the human lifespan is increasing; thus, these prisoners will simply live longer in our care. We have not addressed the additional health care needs and the geriatric issues that are associated with longer life.

Our current reality restricts our ability to think outside the paradigm box, and to create innovative and effective interventions for the youth population prevalent in our adult systems. As such, our educational, vocational, counseling, spiritual, health, and recreational programs are a duplication of what currently exists in the juvenile justice arena, or that which has been retrofitted for the adult justice system. We are incapacitated to look beyond the horizon and envision what may be possible to habilitate these youthful offenders so they can assume constructive roles in their communities as they return home after they serve their court-imposed sanctions.

Yet, there are incremental changes that have occurred in our systems that allow glimpses of alternative ways to handle juveniles in adult correctional systems. Toward that end, there are strategies we may employ to help stretch our paradigms and force us beyond our natural comfort zones, to create better, more effective and efficient models to deal with the youthful offender.

Creating the Future

The future is ours to invent. If we believe that we can make a better system in which we will provide safety to our communities, and protect our communities from violence, aggression, and crime, then we must direct our energies to change what currently exists. We recognize that we as a profession, as an industry, and as a system can do things differently. We have witnessed these alternate paradigms as we have conducted our own work throughout the United States, Canada, and abroad.

We have seen the Women's Institution in Shakopee, Minnesota—a maximum-security facility, set in a small urban area, with no fence, no razor ribbon wire, across from a municipal park and an elementary school—operate with no escapes in their recent history. We have observed Colorado reinvent their youth offender system, with no new resources, to provide a developmental youth-oriented habilitation system within the context of an adult system. We have examined how South Carolina has pioneered techniques for youth offenders who were traditionally rejected by adult correctional systems, within the standard operating procedures of adult institutions. We have witnessed the state of Washington devote minimal resources to engage county probation departments to provide cognitive intervention programs for offenders, thereby reducing recidivism and maximizing cost effectiveness. We have seen how the state of Louisiana has incorporated adolescent development principles into a youth development system for all juvenile institutions throughout their state.

How do these jurisdictions, by example, begin to change what is to what could be? What are some of the tactics that others may use to accomplish system change? These changes may be made at all levels. Changes can be made by the chief executive officer of the jurisdiction, a chief administrator of an institution or community corrections program, a manager, a supervisor, or a direct care worker (correctional officer, teacher, counselor, cook, secretary, to name but a few). All staff should be encouraged to take responsibility for system change and adopt tactics to accomplish that goal, if that is the system's direction.

1. **Create a vision.** The first step is to create and publish your vision. While it is generally perceived that it is the chief executive officer who creates and sets the vision for the system, all members of the system have an integral part to play in the dream. Indeed, interaction among staff and groups within the organization set the climate and tone for the development of a vision. What is a vision? It is the dream. It is not unlike a mission statement for an organization, except it has elements of incremental accomplishments that are possible to achieve with hard work and coordinated effort. The vision is the unfettered view of what can be, unencumbered by what is or what is not possible. It is to dream a dream of possibility, even though it may not seem like reality at the moment. It is ideal, yet real; profound, yet not complex; perfect, yet achievable; it is exemplary, yet ordinary. The vision is the framework toward which your paradigm is compared. It fosters change and challenges ingenuity.

   Once we have a vision, we must publish it. We do not mean just to write it down. We must advertise it. This means speaking about it at staff meetings, encouraging discussion about it, engaging youth to think about it, and yes, even taking every opportunity to quote it in our daily correspondence.

2. **Write a future history.** Once we have a vision and have published it, we must begin to achieve that vision. Begin with writing a different kind of history. Those who study history know that we look at events retrospectively. That means that we look back at the event and create the story that led to its occurrence. Once we have a vision, we

should look at it as if it were already a historical event and write a prospective story. That is, write the story that must take place in order for the event to occur. The difficulty of this task is that the inventor of a future event must reach beyond the reality of any existing paradigm. The authors of a future history must be comfortable reaching beyond the boundaries of their existing paradigm window, looking at what has not yet occurred, and creating it. The futurists create the events, envisioning them first in their mind, and then insuring that they happen. Writing a future history is a difficult, but not impossible, task. When accomplished, it frees staff to achieve what before was thought to be impossible.

3. **Identify the barriers to accomplish the future.** After writing the future history, staff should be encouraged to identify all the barriers that they perceive will hinder that future from being achieved. This is when the pragmatic reality of daily operations may prove beneficial. It is here that the barriers to achieve the future are recorded. We suggest that there be no debate, nor any discussion on the merits of the barriers suggested. Instead, it should be a brainstormed list of what may be, not what is. Toward that end, the barriers, as suggested, provide the correctional staff with opportunities to direct their energy towards the foundation for fundamental systems change. This list, along with the next, is fundamental to the future that we wish to create.

4. **Identify the supports to accomplish the future.** Staff also should be encouraged to identify all the supports available to accomplish the future vision and future history that has been identified. Here, also, staff is encouraged to create a brainstormed list with no debate or discussion as to the merits of the suggestions made. Indeed, both this and the previous lists will be discussed, challenged, and refined to create the future history as written. The supports that are available are typical. They include administrative events such as policy direction, budget and resource availability, personnel, and program design. Staff should be encouraged to stretch their paradigms to include supports that are not traditional. These may be such activities as community involvement, spiritual interventions, stakeholder endorsements, and political ratification, to name but a few.

5. **Create the Plan.** The future history plan is unlike any we have described thus far either in this or previous work. It is not a management plan. It is not an implementation plan, nor does it include the typical components of an operational plan. Rather, the plan is the future history narrative. It is the step-by-step story of how the event happened, not from the historical perspective (in other words, looking back at the event) but from the future perspective (looking forward). This is the story that is told

and begins: "Once upon a time." It is an opening scene of *Star Wars Episode IV*, or any *Star Trek* program. It is not the mission statement, but the vision of the future. It is the story told to get to that future.

6. **Implement the Plan.** This step is the actual implementation of the plan based on the story that you have told to accomplish the vision, the dream, the future. Indeed, if you have gotten this far and are still reading, you have a glimpse of what the future may portend and how to achieve it. Congratulations! You have been able to conceive outside the safety of your existing paradigm. You now have a glimpse of what is possible. It is a beginning.

New Learning, New Beginnings

The *FBI Crime Statistics Report* (November, 1999) was released with some amazing, unexpected data. The FBI reported a 10 percent decrease in serious crimes reported to police in the first half of 1999. The largest decrease was in burglaries (14 percent), followed by murders (13 percent), and auto thefts (12 percent). Murder in cities under 100,000 population dropped a dramatic 25 percent, while it increased by 1 percent in cities over one million. Other remarkable declines included robberies (10 percent); rape (8 percent); aggravated assaults (7 percent); and larceny (8 percent).

As expected, various constituencies are providing their own interpretation for such remarkable results, each taking credit for its own political and/or social agenda. For example, the Clinton administration claimed that the decrease in violent crime was due to their policy on community policing and gun control restrictions. The Republican legislators stated that it was their tougher sentencing laws and ambitious agenda to build more prison cells to incarcerate the most violent serious offenders. As reported on MSNBC's website (http://www.msnbc.com, 11/22/99), criminologists such as James Alan Fox of Northeastern University and Alfred Blumstein of Carnegie Mellon University have begun to analyze this data. They suggest that some of the factors contributing to the decline in violent crime include a reverse-contagion effect of the ordinary citizen where "lawfulness is becoming the norm"; community policing programs that are beginning to impact neighborhood culture; crime prevention and antigun efforts by federal and local authorities; and smaller communities that are taking proactive action against criminals and their activities.

In an MSNBC News Poll (November 21, 1999), of 4,256 responders, 20 percent stated that the reduction in serious crime was due to longer prison sentences; 10 percent thought improved police work was the significant factor; 12 percent believed demographic changes caused the reduced crime rate; and only 4 percent thought gun control was the primary contributing factor. However, 54 percent of those polled thought that a strong economy was the primary factor influencing and reducing the serious crime rate. In times of a weaker economy, it will be instructive to notice what happens to the crime rate.

We are encouraged by the crime statistics reported by the Federal Bureau of Investigation. We are even more optimistic that the general population has begun to consider a variety of factors that may contribute to lower crime rates. Now, it is up to the corrections professions to help the general public to focus on the alternatives to harsh punishment for violent youthful offenders. It offers us a new beginning, because once the general public begins to understand the factors that have been introduced by Andrews, Gendreau, Latessa, Goldstein, Glick, and others, then we can begin to help focus the politicians toward a constructive national youth policy.

What is some of the new learning we can use as we change our current reality and manage our systems to deal effectively with youthful offenders placed in adult corrections systems?

- It will take a multimodal response to effect change in youthful offender behavior. We must address and account for crime prevention, crime intervention, crime suppression, as well as developmental and social factors.
- A number of interconnected factors must be identified and managed to reduce criminal behavior among youth. These include education, vocational training, health services, spiritual and religious needs, job placement, and consistent community supervision after institutional release.
- Criminal behavior is not impacted by any one factor, but must be confronted by a multiplicity of factors including: drug and gun control; accountability for antisocial behavior; alternatives to incarceration; community supervision programs; police involvement in routine community affairs; support from neighborhoods and community involvement; strong educational and vocational support systems; mentoring programs during and after incarceration; primary prevention programs before youth begin to engage in criminal behaviors; youth programs and groups; active involvement with community and social projects.
- The community must coalesce around its youth as they begin to engage in antisocial experimentation. We learn from the Boys and Girls Clubs (*see* Glick and Rhine, 2001) and Big Brothers, Big Sisters Programs that there are viable interventions for at-risk youths, even those considered violent criminals.
- Harsh punishment does not reduce crime in and of itself. However, when combined with program interventions that meet youths' development needs and sound adolescent principles of growth, criminal behavior can be reduced dramatically.
- There needs to be a coordinated, integrated effort to have an impact on youthful offender behavior. This includes planning and program implementation that cuts

across traditional lines of authority and system interventions. Youths must perceive caring and concerned adults in a seamless continuity of services, programs, and community.

- Primary prevention programs are more effective and cost efficient than secondary prevention programs; and secondary prevention programs are more effective and cost efficient than tertiary prevention programs. Any of these interventions are more effective than merely punishment or incarceration programs.
- The criminal justice systems are capable of positive, effective, and efficient youthful offender interventions, with minimal additional resources.

A Final Thought

It is our hope that we have provided a blueprint to manage and implement effective youth offender programs within adult correctional systems. As with any guide, the suggestions are only as good as your perception that they are realistic, they can be implemented, and they will make a difference. We believe what we have offered meets these basic criteria. More importantly, we have attempted to provide a framework for action. We wanted to incite thought, create an atmosphere of challenge and opportunity, and provoke action based not on where the systems are currently, but their potential as to where they can be. If we have accomplished that much, then we have met our objective for this monograph.

We are optimistic that appropriate change can occur to better meet the needs of the youthful offender placed in our adult correctional systems. We are optimistic because the theory has been developed, the technology is available, and the willingness to make a change has been demonstrated. As we have stated before: we are pioneer authors as we implement this social policy. We challenge all correctional staff, from aide to administrator, from correctional officer to commissioner, from trainer and teacher, to technician, to citizens, to take up the gauntlet and together improve the treatment of juveniles in adult facilities.

REFERENCES

Able, G. G., J. V. Becker, W. D. Murphy, and B. Flanagan. 1981. Identifying Dangerous Child Molesters. In R. Stuart, ed. *Violent Behaviors: Social Learning Approaches to Prediction, Management, and Treatment.* New York: Brunner/Mazel.

Agee, V. M. 1996. Treatment of Youthful Sex Offenders in Adult Institutions. In *Managing Violent Youthful Offenders in Adult Corrections Systems.* Longmont, Colorado: National Institute of Corrections.

Agency for Health Care Policy and Research. 1994. Clinical Practice Guideline No. 9. Management of Cancer Pain. Rockville, Maryland: U.S. Department of Health and Human Services, March.

Altschuler, D. M. and T. L. Armstrong. 1991. Intensive Aftercare for the High Risk Juvenile Parolee. In T. L. Armstrong, ed. *Intensive Interventions with High Risk Youths.* Monsey, New York: Willow Tree Press, Inc.

———. 1995. Managing Aftercare Services for Delinquents. In B. Glick and A. P. Goldstein, eds. *Managing Delinquency Programs that Work.* Lanham, Maryland: American Correctional Association.

Amnesty International. 1998. *Betraying the Young: Human Rights Violations Against Children in the United States Justice System.* New York: Amnesty International.

Andrews, D. and J. Bonta. 1994. *The Psychology of Criminal Contact.* Cincinnati, Ohio: Anderson Press.

Andrews, D. , J. Bonta, and R. Hoge. 1990. Classification for Effective Rehabilitation: Rediscovering Psychology. *Criminal Justice and Behavior.* 17, 19-52.

Andrews, D. and J. J. Kiessling. 1980. Program Structure and Effective Correctional Practices: A Summary of the CAVIC Research. In R. R. Ross and P. Gendreau, eds. *Effective Correctional Treatment.* Toronto, Canada: Butterworths. pp. 441-463.

Andrews, D. A., I. Zinger, R. D. Hoge, J. Bonta, P. Gendreau, and F. T. Cullen. 1990. Does Correctional Treatment Work? A Clinically Relevant and Psychologically Informed Meta-analysis. *Criminology.* 28: 369-404.

Apter, S. and A. P. Goldstein. 1986. *Troubled Children: Troubled Systems.* New York: Pergamon Press.

Austin, James, Dedel Kelly Johnson, and Maria Gregoriou. 2000. *Juveniles in Adult Prisons and Jails: A National Assessment.* Institute on Crime, Justice and Corrections at the George

Washington University and the National Council on Crime and Delinquency. Washington, D.C., Bureau of Justice Assistance.

Barker, Joel. 1992. *Paradigms*. Louisville, Kentucky: Harper Business.

Bradley, J. and M. Rotheram. 1989. *Assessment and Suicide Risk among Adolescents: A Training Manual for Runaway Shelter Staff.* Unpublished curriculum.

Brent, D. A., et al. 1988. Risk Factors for Adolescent Suicide. *General Psychiatry*. 45: June.

———. 1993. Psychiatric Risk Factors for Adolescent Suicide: A Case Control Study. *Journal of the American Academy of Adolescent Psychiatry*. 27:362-66.

Brown, J. and P. Langan. 1994. *State Court Sentencing of Convicted Felons*. Washington, D.C.: Bureau of Justice Statistics.

Brown, L. K. 1991. The Correlates of Planning in Adolescent Suicide Attempts. *Journal of the American Academy of Child and Adolescent Psychiatry*. 30: 95-99.

Brown, Lou. 1991. *Critical Issues in the Lives of People with Severe Disabilities*. Baltimore: P. N. Brookes.

Bureau of Justice Statistics. 1998. *School Crime Supplement 1989 and 1995: An Analysis*. Washington, D.C.: U.S. Department of Justice.

———. October 2000. *Juveniles in Adult Prisons and Jails: A National Assessment*. Washington, D.C.: U.S. Department of Justice.

Bush, J. M. and B. Bilodeau. 1993. *Options: A Cognitive Change Program*. Longmont, Colorado: National Institute of Corrections.

Butts, J. and G. Halemba. 1994. Delays in Juvenile Justice Findings from a National Survey. *Juvenile and Family Court Journal*. 33.

Calloway, J. 1995. Managing Recreation and Leisure for Juvenile Delinquents. In B. Glick and A. P. Goldstein, eds. *Managing Delinquency Programs that Work*. Lanham, Maryland: American Correctional Association.

Cellini, H., B. Schwartz, and S. Readio. 1993. Child Sexual Abuse: An Administrator's Nightmare. In *School Safety Update*. Westlake Village, California: National School Safety Center.

Clear, T. R. 1995. The Design and Implementation of Classifications Systems. *Federal Probation*. 59(2): 58-61.

Commission on Corrections Court Review. 1969. Washington, D.C.: U.S. Commission on Corrections.

Davis, Sue. 1992. Power on the Court: Chief Justice Rehnquist's Opinion Assignments. In Elliot E. Slotnick, ed. *Judicial Politics: Readings from the Judicature*. Chicago: Nelson-Hall Publishers.

Drapkin, Martin. 1996. *Developing Policies and Procedures for Jails*. Lanham, Maryland: American Correctional Association.

Ewing, C. P. 1990. *Kids Who Kill*. Boston, Massachusetts: Houghton Mifflin.

Fayol, H. 1949. *General and Industrial Management*. New York: Pitman.

Federal Bureau of Investigation. 1974, 1995, 1997, 1998, 1999. *Uniform Crime Reports*. Washington, D.C.: U.S. Department of Justice.

———. 1999. *Crime Report*. November. Washington, D.C.: U.S. Department of Justice.

Feindler, E. L. 1979. *Cognitive and Behavioral Approaches to Anger Control Training in Explosive Adolescents*. Unpublished doctoral dissertation. West Virginia University.

Feindler, E. L., S. A. Marriott, and M. Iwata. 1984. Group Anger Control Training for Junior High School Delinquents. *Cognitive Therapy and Research*. 8: 299-311.

Finnigan, J. 1995. *Societal Outcomes of Drug and Alcohol Treatment in the State of Oregon–Phase One Report*. Eugene, Oregon: Oregon Department of Substance Abuse Services.

Fox, James A. and Marianne W. Zawitz. March 2000. *Homicide Trends in the United States: 1988 Update*. Crimes Data Brief. Washington, D.C.: Bureau of Justice.

Gendreau, P., D. A. Andrews. 1994. *The Correctional Program Assessment Inventory (4th Edition)*. Saint John, New Brunswick: University of New Brunswick.

Gendreau, P., F. T. Cullen, and J. Bonta. 1994. Intensive Rehabilitation Supervision: The Next Generation in Community Corrections. *Federal Probation*. 58: 72-78.

Gendreau, P., M. Paparozzi, T. Little, and M. Goddard. 1993. Punishing Smarter: The Effectiveness of the New Generation of Alternative Sanctions. *Forum on Correctional Research*. 5:31-34.

Gendreau, P. and R. R. Ross. 1983-84. Correctional Treatment: Some Recommendations for Successful Intervention. *Juvenile and Family Court Journal*. 34:31-40.

Gilmore, T. and R. Nelson. 1978. Responsibility Charting in Corrections. *Federal Probation*. 1978:6.

Glick, B. 1979. Youth Between the Cracks. *Behavioral Disorders*. Vol. 4, No. 4. August: 227-230.

———. 1986. Programming for Juvenile Delinquents: An Administrator's Perspective. In S. J. Apter and A. P. Goldstein, eds. *Youth Violence: Programs and Prospects*. Elmsford, New York: Pergamon Press.

Glick, B. and A.P. Goldstein, eds. 1995. *Managing Delinquency Programs that Work*. Lanham, Maryland: American Correctional Association.

Glick, B. and E. Rhine, eds. 2001. *Journal of Correctional Best Practices: Juveniles in Adult Correctional Systems*. Lanham, Maryland: American Correctional Association.

Glick, B. and W. Sturgeon. 1998. *No Time to Play: Youthful Offenders in Adult Correctional Systems*. Lanham, Maryland: American Correctional Association.

Glueck, S. and I. Glueck. 1950. *Unraveling Juvenile Delinquency*. New York: Commonwealth Fund.

Goldstein, A. P. and B. Glick. 1987. *Aggression Replacement Training: A Comprehensive Intervention for Aggressive Youth*. Champaign, Illinois: Research Press.

———. 1989. *Reducing Delinquency: Intervention in the Community*. New York: Pergamon Press.

———. 1994. *The Prosocial Gang: Implementing Aggression Replacement Training*. Thousand Oaks, California: Sage Publications.

———. 1983. Juvenile Delinquency. In A.P. Goldstein, ed. *The Prevention and Containment of Aggression*. Elmsford, New York: Pergamon Press.

Goldstein, A. P. and G. Segal. 1983. *Aggression in Global Perspective*. Elmsford, New York: Pergamon Press.

Grisso, Thomas and Robert G. Schwartz, eds. 2000. *Youth on Trial: A Developmental Perspective on Juvenile Justice*. Chicago: University of Chicago Press.

Gullick, L. F. 1943. *The Elements of Administration*. New York: Harper and Row.

Hayes, L. M. and J. R. Rowan. 1989. *National Study of Jail Suicides: Seven Years Later*. Alexandria, Virginia: National Center on Institutions and Alternatives.

Hendrin, H. 1986. Suicide: A Review of New Directions in Research. *Hospital Community Psychiatry*. 37: 148-154.

Hersey, P. and K. Blanchard. 1977. *Organizational Change through Effective Leadership*. New York: Prentice Hall.

———. 1985. *The Situational Leader*. Escondido, California: Center for Leadership.

Hirschi, T. 1969. *Causes of Delinquency*. Newbury Park, California: Sage Publications.

Howard, John. 1792 (1973). *The State of Prisons, 4th Edition*. Montclair, New Jersey: Patterson-Smith.

Hurst, Hunter. 1989. The Death Penalty for Juveniles. *Juvenile and Family Court Newsletter*. Vol. 19, No. 6.

Jackson, Lonnie. 1998. *Gangbusters: Strategies for Prevention and Intervention*. Lanham, Maryland: American Correctional Association.

Jacobs, D. G. 1989. Evaluation and Care of Suicidal Behavior in Emergency Settings. In D. G. Jacobs and H. N. Brown, eds. *Suicide: Understanding and Responding*. Harvard Medical School Perspectives on Suicide. Madison, Connecticut: International Universities Press.

Latessa, E. 1997. *Corrections in the Community*. Chapel Hill, North Carolina: Baker Books.

Latessa, E. and G. Vito, 1989. *Statistical Applications in Criminal Justice*. Thousand Oaks, California: Sage Publications.

Levinson, Robert. 1999. *Unit Management in Prisons and Jails*. Lanham, Maryland: American Correctional Association.

Lipsey, M. W. 1992. Juvenile Delinquency Treatment: A Meta-analytic Inquiry into the Variability of Effects. In T. D. Cook, ed. *Meta Analysis for Explanation: A Casebook*. New York: Russell Sage Foundation.

Locke, John. 1980. Paternal Power. In C. B. MacPherson, ed. *Second Treatise of Government*. Indianapolis, Indiana: Hackett Publishing Co.

Lyons, J. 1994. *Inmate Suicide Report.* New York: New York State Department of Correctional Services.

Marcus, P., et al. 1993. Characteristics of Suicides by Inmates in an Urban Jail. *Hospital and Community Psychiatry.* 44: 3.

Marstellar, F. 1995. *Mental Disorders among Youth in Georgia Detention Facilities.* Atlanta, Georgia: Emory University Research Project.

Martinson, R. 1974. What Works? Questions and Answers about Prison Reform. *The Public Interest.* 36:22-45.

Marttunen, M. J., et al. 1994. Psychological Stressors More Common in Adolescent Suicides with Alcohol Abuses Compared with Depressive Adolescent Suicides. *Journal of the American Academy of Child and Adolescent Psychiatry.* 33:4, May.

Meichenbaum, D. 1977. *Cognitive Behavior Modification.* New York: Plenum Press.

Meichenbaum, D., B. Gilmore, and A. Fedoravicius. 1971. Group Insight vs. Group Desensitization in Treating Speech Anxiety. *Journal of Consulting and Clinical Psychology.* 36, 410-421.

National Center for Juvenile Justice. 2001. *Easy Access to Juvenile Court Statistics: 1988-1997.* Pittsburgh, Pennsylvania: National Center for Juvenile Justice.

National Youth Gang Center. 1997. *National Youth Gang Survey: Program Summary.* Washington, D.C.: U.S. Department of Justice, Office of Juvenile Justice and Delinquency Prevention.

New York State Division for Youth. 1996. *Technical Report.* Rensselaer, New York: Division for Youth.

Novaco, R. W. 1975. *Anger Control: The Development and Evaluation of an Experimental Treatment.* Lexington, Massachusetts: Lexington Books.

———. 1979. Anger and Coping with Stress. In J. Foreyt and D. Rathjen, eds. *Cognitive Behavior Therapy: Therapy, Research and Practice.* New York: Plenum Press.

Office of Juvenile Justice and Delinquency Prevention. November, 2000. *Comprehensive Responses to Youth at Risk: Interim Findings from the Safe Futures Initiative,* and OJJDP Summary. Washington, D.C.: Office of Juvenile Justice and Delinquency Prevention.

———. 2000. 1998 *National Youth Gang Survey (Summary)*. November. Washington, D.C.: Office of Juvenile Justice and Delinquency Prevention.

O'Leary, V. and T. R. Clear. 1995. *Community Corrections into the 21st Century*. Washington, D.C.: National Institute of Corrections.

Parent, Dale, et al. 1994. *Conditions of Confinement: Juvenile Detention and Corrections Facilities*. Washington, D.C.: Office of Juvenile Justice and Delinquency Prevention.

Pederson, P. 1988. *A Handbook for Developing Multicultural Awareness*. Alexandria, Virginia: American Counseling Association.

Puritz, P. and Mary Ann Scali. January 1998. *Beyond the Walls: Improving Conditions of Confinement for Youth in Custody*. Washington, D.C.: Office of Juvenile Justice and Delinquency Prevention.

Puzzanchera, Charles, et al. May 2000. *Juvenile Court Statistics 1997*. Washington, D.C.: National Center for Juvenile Justice. Office of Juvenile Justice and Delinquency Prevention.

Redl, F. and D. Wineman. 1957. *Aggressive Child*. New York: Free Press.

Ross, R., E. Fabiano, and R. Ross. 1986. *Reasoning and Rehabilitation: A Handbook for Teaching Cognitive Skills*. Ottawa, Ontario, Canada: The Cognitive Center.

Schwartz, B. K. and H. R. Cellini, eds. 1995. *The Sex Offender: Corrections, Treatment and Legal Practice*. Kingston, New Jersey: Civic Research Institute, Inc.

Sely, H. 1956. *The Stress of Life*. New York: McGraw-Hill Book Company.

Shaffer D., et al. 1974. Suicide in Children and Early Adolescents. *Journal of Psychology and Psychiatry*. 15: 275-91.

Shafi, M., et al. 1985. Psychological Autopsy of Completed Suicide in Children and Adolescents. *Journal of Clinical Psychiatry*. 142:1061-64.

Soriano, F. I. 1993. Cultural Sensitivity and Gang Intervention. In A. P. Goldstein and C. R. Huff, eds. *The Gang Intervention Handbook*. Champaign, Illinois: Research Press.

———. 1995. Cultural Sensitivity in Delinquency Prevention and Intervention Programs. In B. Glick and A. P. Goldstein, eds. *Managing Delinquency Programs that Work*. Lanham, Maryland: American Correctional Association.

Stahl, Ann, et al. May, 2000. *Juvenile Court Statistics, 1997.* Washington, D.C.: National Center for Juvenile Justice.

Sturgeon, W. 1993. *Gang Intervention Curriculum for Jails.* Longmont, Colorado; National Institute of Corrections.

Sturgeon, W., et al. 1990. *Prison Security Curriculum.* Longmont, Colorado: National Institute of Corrections.

Taylor, B. 1975. *Management Development and Training.* London: McGraw-Hill.

Taymans, J. and S. Parese. 1995. *Problem Solving Skills for Offenders.* Longmont, Colorado: National Institute of Corrections.

Thornberry, T. P. 1994. *Violent Families and Youth Violence. Fact Sheet.* Washington D.C.: U.S. Department of Justice, Office of Justice Programs, Office of Juvenile Justice and Delinquency Prevention.

Thornberry, T. P., A. J. Lizotte, M. D. Krohn, M. Farnwoth, and S. J. Jang. 1991. Testing Interfactional Theory of Reciprocal Causal Relationships among Family, School, and Delinquency. *The Journal of Criminal Law and Criminology.* 82:3-35.

Travis, L. F. and E. J. Latessa. 1996. Classification and Needs Assessment Module. In *Managing Violent Youthful Offenders in Adult Institutions.* Longmont, Colorado: National Institute of Corrections.

Urwick, L. F. 1955. The Purpose of Business. *Dun's Review and Modern Industry.* 52:103-5.

———. 1961. Management and Human Relations. In R. Tannenbaum, ed. *Leadership and Organization: A Behavior Science Approach.* New York: McGraw-Hill.

U.S. Department of Education, and U.S. Department of Justice. 1998. *Annual Report on School Safety,* 1998. Washington, D.C.: U.S. Department of Education, U.S. Department of Justice, Office of Justice Programs, Office of Juvenile Justice and Delinquency Prevention.

U.S. Department of Health and Human Services. 1999. *Mental Health: A Report of the Surgeon General.* National Institute of Mental Health. Washington, D.C.: Government Printing Office.

Utah Department of Corrections. 1994. *Housing Strategies for Serious Youthful Offenders.* Salt Lake City, Utah: Utah Department of Corrections.

Wolfgang, M. 1958. An Analysis of Homicide/Suicide. *Journal of Clinical Experimental Psychopathology*. 19: 208-218.

Yochelson, S. and S. Samenow. 1976. *The Criminal Personality, Vol. I: A Profile for Change*. New York: Jason Aronson.

Zeigler, W. 1973. *Futures Invention*. Syracuse, New York: Unpublished workshop.

INDEX

A

B

C

Recess Is Over

ABOUT THE AUTHORS

Barry Glick received his Ph.D. from Syracuse University in 1972. Trained as a counseling psychologist, Dr. Glick has devoted his professional career to the development of policies, programs, and services for adolescents. His specialization is in juvenile delinquency, aggression, and violence, as well as the emotionally disturbed adolescent. Dr. Glick has worked in both private child care agencies and state government. He has held positions as a child care worker, a psychologist, an administrator, a manager, and an agency executive staffer. Previously holding the post of Associate Deputy Director for Local Services, New York State Division for Youth, he is currently a national consultant to juvenile and adult correctional systems, as Chief Operations Officer of G & G Consultants, LLC. Dr. Glick has published numerous books, chapters, and articles on aggressive and violent youth, youth in corrections, and in juvenile systems. He has been co-editor in chief of the *Journal of Correctional Best Practices*, senior editor of *Managing Delinquency Programs that Work*, and first author of *No Time to Play: Youthful Offenders in Adult Systems*. Dr. Glick holds positions on several editorial boards including the Center for Credentialing and Education, an affiliate of the National Board for Certified Counselors, is a member emeritus of the National Gangs Advisory Committee, and is a nationally certified counselor.

William "Bill" Sturgeon has more than twenty-five years of experience in the criminal justice field. During this time, he has held management positions in both law enforcement and corrections. He is the co-author of *No Time to Play: Youthful Offenders in Adult Correctional Systems*. He has been a consultant for the U.S. House of Representatives, the National Institute of Corrections, numerous state and local governments, the Republic of South Africa, and The Netherlands. Mr. Sturgeon has also consulted for many private companies. Mr. Sturgeon received an associate degree from Berkshire Community College, a bachelor's degree from Southern Vermont College, a master's degree from Goddard College, and training in conflict management and mediation from the Harvard School of Public Health.

Also by the Authors of *Recess is Over*!

No Time to Play: Youthful Offenders in Adult Correctional Systems

Barry Glick, Ph.D. and William Sturgeon, MA
with Charles R. Venator-Santiago

No Time to Play provides the fundamental knowledge for policy makers, administrators, managers, supervisors, and direct line staff to apply to their current and future situations. This resource includes history and a re-evaluation of current thinking. It also provides basic information about adolescent development, and the organization, administration, and management issues that need to be addressed when providing programs and services to the violent youthful offender. Specific programs and services required for violent youthful offenders with special needs are also considered. (1998, 181 pages, index, 1-56991-071-5)

#221-RO • Nonmembers $23.95 • ACA members $18.35

Managing Delinquency Programs That Work

Edited by Barry Glick, Ph.D. and Arnold P. Goldstein, Ph.D.

Juvenile justice practitioners will gain invaluable insight from the sixteen essays included in this resource. Written by experienced professionals, *Managing Delinquency Programs that Work* offers guidance on policy formulation and direction, program development and administration, training and evaluation, and system issues. Explores multicultural training and cross-cultural counseling, managing recreation, recognizing multi-variable training options, developing aftercare services and handling budgeting concerns. In addition, it addresses the issue of devising public relations strategies, recognizing special needs and concerns of the female offender, staffing treatment programs and understanding the role of professional associations in devising effective strategies to manage juvenile delinquency. (1995, 374 pages, index, 1-56991-011-1)

#243-RO • Nonmembers $23.95 • ACA members $18.35

ACA
FOUNDED 1870

To order, call 1-800-222-5646, ext. 1860
American Correctional Association
4380 Forbes Boulevard, Lanham, MD 20706
www.aca.org or www.corrections.com/aca